Reviewers' Comm....

A flurry of recent research into teams and diversity tells us that the most effective and most creative teams are those, which value difference and establish practical ways, in which they can capitalise on the diversity of their members. Unfortunately, putting this wisdom into practice isn't often easy. Karen Jackson and Ian Taylor have captured the mood of this emerging movement in a broad-ranging review of some of the factors that influence how a team manages difference. They provide insights into often hidden and undiscussed areas of team dynamics, such as collective values and differences in approaches to problem-solving and decision-making. This is a well-researched, thought-provoking foray into an area of management which will assume increasing importance in the future, as the quality of team functioning becomes more and more of a differentiating factor between high performing organisations and the rest.

Professor David Clutterbuck

As the owner manager of an SME I am generally sceptical as to the relevance of management texts to an organisation such as mine. Generally I find that the methodologies and techniques described are skewed towards larger corporations and their need to manage and stimulate groups in multiple locations. I was pleasantly surprised to find that the Power of Difference is extremely relevant to my own needs. Rationalising the problems within our teams and repairing those weaknesses has previously been approached empirically. Whereas I now feel confident the techniques identified within the book will allow for a much more systematic approach to solving those weaknesses as they arise.

Tim Johnsen, Managing Director, Eagle Scientific Ltd

I've been through just about every sort of team-building and diversity program known to man during my 25-year tenure with one of the global oil majors. Most were interesting and helpful for a short period of time but their focus was on the usual list of "differences": race, gender, culture, etc. The one standout is the time spent with Ian and Karen. Their message, embodied in this book, goes deeper than the obvious and in so doing creates not only a sustainable foundation for maximizing team members' contribution to the task at hand, but helps teams work out the other differences too. This book will help serious managers maximize the human potential within their teams.

Kent Hill, BP Refining & Marketing Data Architect

Having worked with the authors for over twenty years where they have facilitated workshops for teams that I have managed or been part of, it is really encouraging to see their vast experience distilled into a very readable and practical book on teams and especially the value of diversity in the widest sense of the word, rather than the narrow definition so much in vogue in the early 21st century. This book is a must for any team that is striving to move their performance from good to extraordinary.

A senior IT manager in an international oil company

For a complete list of Management Books 2000 titles
visit our website on http://www.mb2000.com

THE POWER OF DIFFERENCE

*Karen Jackson &
Ian Taylor*

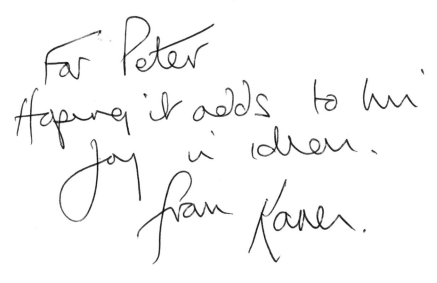

For Peter
Hoping it adds to his
joy in idleness.
from Karen.

2000

First published in 2008 by Management Books 2000 Ltd
Forge House, Limes Road
Kemble, Cirencester
Gloucestershire, GL7 6AD, UK
Tel: 0044 (0) 1285 771441
Fax: 0044 (0) 1285 771055
Email: info@mb2000.com
Web: www.mb2000.com

British Library Cataloguing in Publication Data is available

ISBN 9781852525491

Acknowledgements

This book is the result of our work as consultants for a wide range of organisations over the last twenty years and we would like to thank all those people who have helped to shape our ideas. In particular, we are grateful to Mark Brown, who introduced us to 'thinking afresh', Dr Michael Kirton, who developed our ideas on cognitive style and diversity, and David Casey, who made us think about the behavioural differences between groups and teams.

Over the years we've spent within DEVA we have been fortunate in working with a number of gifted colleagues and would especially like to recognise the support of Nigel Barlow, Robert Maguire and Janet Izatt. We would also like to thank our editor, Michael Ayton.

Contents

9

Contents

1

Introduction

What is this book about?

Teams exist to achieve the objectives of the organisation, in situations where the scale of the problem has grown beyond an individual's competence or ability. Many of the problems dealt with by teams are problems that have occurred before and to which there are tried and trusted solutions. In other cases, groups of people are faced by problems that no one has experienced before. Problems are as numerous as teams themselves. As the subtitle of this book suggests, however, the resources that a team has for solving its problems can be explored much more deeply, and in such a way as to reveal the value and brilliance of the diversity within the team. This book is a celebration of difference and a paean to the complexity of human nature and its ability to solve whatever problem is thrown at it, as attested by the fact that we have existed and evolved over thousands of years.

Each individual wants to be valued for what they can bring to the team's problem-solving capacity. It is this human hunger to be valued which is itself part of the value of diversity. Being valued creates self-respect, psychological well-being and enhanced performance. If someone is different from other members of the team in ways that we describe in the book, it is possible that their contribution will not be understood or appreciated as much as it could and should be, and that as a result it will not be valued. One of the aims of this book is to show that, in certain circumstances, it is these individual differences that can determine the success or otherwise of the team. If people who are different from other team members have the confidence to know that they have something to offer, they will not only make more of a contribution but also help others to do the same. The important thing to register is that we are all different in one way or another. If everyone is allowed to shine, the results will indeed be brilliant.

The success of the car-maker Toyota is due at least in part to its management philosophy, which states that the prime role of a manager is to prepare the next generation of managers, by promoting the talents of everyone in the team. Our hope and belief is that, whether you are the leader of a team or a member of one, reading and acting on the ideas we have explored in this book will make you think about the talent in your team and your place in it and enable you to unlock and exploit a resource which already exists. In order to make your team more effective you need to manage the differences inherent in your team members. This diversity comprises the different ways in which each individual thinks and behaves across a wide spectrum of work situations. This is a big claim. But the ingredients are already to hand – all you have to do is know about the diversity factors, understand when they can be applied appropriately (and when they are acting against you), and use them to the best advantage.

Diversity in the workplace is commonly seen as comprising differences in age, gender, race, ethnicity, colour and religion. These areas of diversity are certainly important and relevant, although they are usually described in terms of how individuals interact, and of how they affect an individual's relationship with the organisation (i.e. in relation to equal opportunities), rather than in terms of their bearing on team behaviour and team effectiveness.[1] What is seldom discussed in terms of team diversity is the issue of differences in areas such as cognitive style (problem-solving and creative thinking), team role preferences, values, national cultures, masculine and feminine approaches, ethics and technology, and how these differences can affect how a team operates, either negatively or positively – in other words, how these variables affect how effective a team can be. We agree with the definition offered by the Chartered Institute of Personnel and Development (CIPD):

> Diversity is ... the concept that people should be valued as individuals for reasons related to business interests, as well as for

moral and social reasons. It recognises that people … can bring fresh ideas and perceptions which can make the way work is done more efficient and products and services better.[2]

In this book, we will focus on problem-solving in teams.

There is another reason why we should be paying more attention to diversity in general, but particularly at work. Working with others from around the globe is now commonplace within multinational organisations, and it is here in these teams that many important problems are being solved which affect us all. Howard Gardner (currently number 70 in *Prospect* magazine's list of the world's top hundred intellectuals) names 'the respectful mind' as one of the five minds individuals need to be able to function well in the future.[3] He says that 'the respectful mind' welcomes differences between people, tries to understand others and seeks to work effectively with them. It is not just 'a nice to have'; it is a necessity for the global village. We feel we can build on this idea by exploring ways that you, the manager or team member, can do these things.

One of the questions you may want to ask is why we have stressed the word 'power' in our book. We believe that 'power is the ability to act'. After reading this book you may choose to act or you may not, but you have the ability to do so, which in itself is very powerful. The book is a combination of ideas – to convince you that there is an argument, and get you thinking about your own team – and practical suggestions, including exercises, about what you can do. Not everything in the book will apply to you and your team, and you can pick your way through the bits that do. You have the power.

To summarise, this book sets out to explore these two issues:

1. How diversity in all its forms (not just the equal opportunities focus on age, gender, race, ethnic origin, colour and religion) affects team behaviour.

2. How this diversity can be understood and used positively to make teams more effective, especially in situations where they are facing shared or unshared uncertainty.

We are *not* saying that diversity is the *only* issue you need to address

15

to make a team effective. That would be nonsense. There are a great many things you have to do to make sure that the team operates well – what has been called 'the discipline of team basics',[4] for example. We *are* saying that there is a hidden group of dimensions within your team that might be hindering you if ignored, but could enhance your team effectiveness exponentially if you knew about them and could exploit them. We are not using the word 'exploit' here in any malign sense. We are making the assumption that having a more effective team, which uses everyone's skills appropriately, is not only good for you and the organisation, but good for the team members themselves, in terms of self-respect, achievement and psychological well-being.

You may already have some questions as a result of reading these opening paragraphs, such as:

• Why do I have to use my energy to get my team to work together? Why do individuals in teams not work together more harmoniously on their own and produce better results?

• Does it matter what type of team it is or what the team objectives are? Will team members' using their diversity make a difference to how they behave whatever the situation?

• What sort of diversity are we talking about? Does my team have to include all the diversities that there are? Do I need to understand and use all these diversities all of the time?

And perhaps many more. We will explore all these questions in Chapter 2.

Trust and openness

We are firmly of the opinion that trust and openness can contribute to the success of a team, especially where there is uncertainty relative either to the nature of the problem to be solved or to its outcome, or both. The amount of trust or uncertainty in the team is something which all team leaders and members need to think about and which we will be discussing at length in the next chapter when we look at the work of David Casey.[5] At this stage, however, we want to raise it

16

from the point of view of the sort of actions you might want to take as a result of reading this book. All managers and leaders want to change the thinking and behaviour of their teams so that they align what team members want with what the organisation wants. This is probably one of the most difficult jobs a manager has to do, especially in times of change. However, the amount of change you can effect depends on the existing level of trust in your group or team – how much its members trust you and how much they trust each other. If trust is high you can work more quickly and cover more ground. If trust is low then you have to work more slowly until you get a level of trust which enables you to go further and faster. We are not talking about camaraderie here. Most teams have that. We are talking about the genuine ability to discuss unpleasant issues openly and reasonably objectively, rather than muttering them behind someone's back. The following model is a good way of looking at this issue.

Johari's Window

Johari's Window sheds light on behaviours in many different circumstances and we use it later in the book when we are discussing values (Chapter 6). The model was devised by Joseph Luft and Harry Ingham in the 1960s, and provides a framework for sharing and disclosing information which we know about ourselves and others and discovering information which others know about us (known and not known to self, and known and not known to others), as Figure 1 shows.

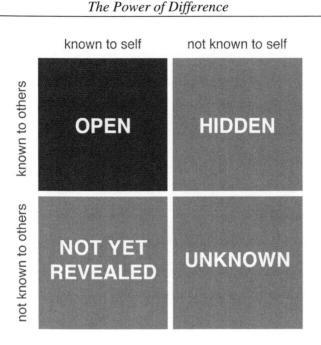

Figure 1. Johari's Window

The figure is based on the idea of a window with four panes of glass which can change their size. In the 'Open' window are issues that are known to us and known to others. They are indeed out in the open. We love sugar in our coffee, and every time we spoon it into the mug that is obvious to everyone else as well. However, we also know things about ourselves which we may not want to share, or will only share when we feel confident that we will not be made fools of or disapproved of. When you first meet someone you might not want to reveal everything about yourself to them, but as your friendship grows you will start to share things. Such things might be unusual hobbies, tastes and skills. The same dynamic is present in teams at work. This box is called 'Not yet revealed'. However, there are also things that people know about you that are not obvious to you. Some of these might be easily observable, but others perhaps come from your reputation or from working with you, such as the fact that you take extensive coffee breaks. Over time, people in your team might share these things with you. Sometimes when we have administered a questionnaire individual team members will say that the results do not reflect their behaviour. We then ask the group to comment on whether it agrees with the questionnaire results or not. Quite often it will agree with the results of the questionnaire rather than with the individual colleague. This box is called 'Hidden'. Finally, there are things that neither side knows. This box is labelled 'Unknown'. This pane might not be revealed until something happens which causes you and your colleagues to develop a greater awareness of your own value and contribution to the team – for example, something which brings out your leadership style.

The less trust and sharing there is in the group, the more it will constrict the 'Open' part of the model. All the other parts become correspondingly greater, as can be seen in Figure 2.

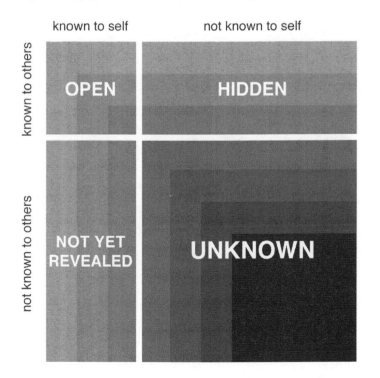

Figure 2. Johari's Window: less trust and openness

This can lead to all sorts of problems in the team, including lack of communication, anger and frustration. It is especially the case if individuals keep important information to themselves because it gives them a feeling of power or an advantage over others.

Conversely, where there is more trust and sharing the 'Open' part of the model grows and the 'Hidden', 'Not yet revealed' and 'Unknown' parts become correspondingly smaller, as shown in Figure 3.

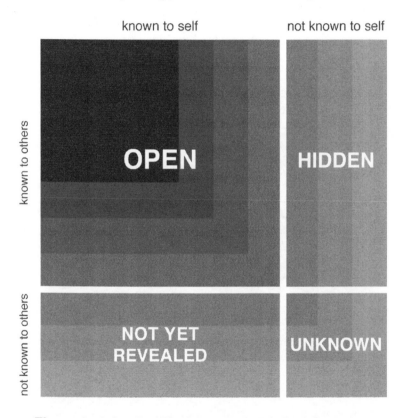

known to self   **not known to self**

known to others

OPEN   **HIDDEN**

not known to others

NOT YET REVEALED   **UNKNOWN**

Figure 3. Johari's Window: more trust and openness

As the leader or manager of a team you have to decide what size the 'Open' pane needs to be. You might decide that the task you are doing does not require much trust and openness and that therefore this is not an issue for you. Many writers on teams feel that this is acceptable, as we describe later in Chapter 2, and indeed in many cases it is. However, even if your team is in a steady state, there may be a requirement in the future for changes to take place and you may ask yourself if your team has the skills to face this challenge. If you can see change on the horizon it may be prudent to start to build up trust ready for the day when it might be needed. In order to help you determine where your team are in terms of the help they need, we have included an exercise for you to complete (Exercise 1, page 227). You can also complete it when you have introduced any of the ideas in this book to the team. You can use it as a benchmark to see if you have made a difference.

Valuing individuals

We have already stated how important it is for each person in a team to feel valued for their contribution. People are insufficiently valued for many reasons, including the fact that they may have a different thinking style or behaviours from others. This may be a useful attribute in some circumstances, as they will not be guilty of 'group think'. The following four-box model entitled 'Roles people play' (Figure 4) demonstrates how people can be wrongly categorised when they have a contribution to make.[6]

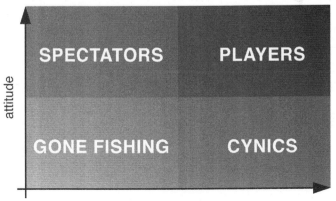

Figure 4. Roles people play

When our team members are seen as having lots of energy and a positive attitude we regard them as being Players. We would like to have more of them and we would be only too grateful if we could turn those in the other three boxes into Players.

When our team members are seen as having a positive attitude but are very low on energy we call them Spectators. These are the people who are very good at talking about what they can do but never actually get down to doing anything. They are always on the sidelines. You need to ask yourself how much responsibility you have as team leader for their behaviour. What is there about them that stops you calling them to account? Why do you not value their actions? They must be doing something while they work for you. What is it? Could it be that you do not appreciate what it is? Perhaps they spend time relating to other teams, or in your eyes wasting time? But what if they know what other teams are doing, and what they want from your team, better than you do? How could this be useful? In other words, perhaps you do not appreciate their behaviour, which is different from other team members' behaviour, because of the way you are looking at it? Spectators may well have been in play in the past, but something has happened which has confused them and they may need more clarity in their role, which you can give them.

When team members are high on energy but don't have the right attitude we call them Cynics. These are people who are doing a lot of the right thing. Indeed they may be working very hard, but they are also highly sceptical about what changes are taking place and what is being achieved, in such a way as to poison the atmosphere. Haven't we seen it all before? What's new about this time? We may regard these team members as a painful cross to bear, but they could be extremely useful. They really want to believe you. Why can't you convince them? If you could, they would put a lot of energy into whatever you are trying to achieve. What is there about them that is different from the other people in your team? If you can find out what this difference is and harness it you are on your way to having a strong ally. Sometimes just giving them some attention or extra responsibilities, or showing that you trust them, will make them value their contribution more and make them want to be a part of what you want to achieve. This might not happen overnight, but your investment will pay off in the end.

Lastly, we have those people with neither energy nor attitude, who are just sitting this one out hoping not to be noticed. They have 'Gone Fishing'. The people in this box are not aligned with the team's objectives. For whatever reason, their interests lie elsewhere. How can you wake them up from their torpor? Are they waiting for retirement? Could you see them off early? If this is not possible owing to financial constraints, are they actually earning their keep? Any war of attrition is very demanding of energy on your side as well as theirs. Is there, again, some way in which you can make how they are behaving work for you? We hope that reading this book will give you some ideas about how to treat them so that they feel valued and you are rewarded for your efforts.

An example of diversity in a team

You may still not be convinced about how the diversity variables affect team behaviour, so below we describe a fairly simple problem-solving situation which will be familiar to many teams who have been involved in team-building in an outdoor location.

We were working recently with a senior team about their approach to business issues. They were a mixed group of men and women of different nationalities, high achievers in a multinational company, who worked across different continents and different time zones – a virtual team. At one point, a discussion arose as to the efficacy or otherwise of team-building exercises set outdoors.

One woman described just such an exercise, where she was part of a small group tasked with transporting a fixed amount of water over difficult terrain, which included crossing a fast-running river, to a final destination. Many of you will be familiar with this type of exercise. She reported that her team was described by the instructor as the most 'awful', but funniest, team he had observed. They came up with, in his view, the worst ideas, but were extremely efficient in terms of how they carried them out.

At this point, one of her listeners suddenly asked her if there had been a time limit on the exercise. Somewhat surprised, she asked why he was enquiring. 'Because you could have drunk the water and reproduced it at the other end', was his reply.

This idea was received with varying degrees of disgust (her), admiration, amazement and laughter by the assembled group. Clearly most of them would never have come up with this solution. Now, faced with an idea that was outside the paradigm of most of their thinking, they had to decide whether it was not only efficient but acceptable, and therefore effective. Did urine and water equate? Was the water required to make tea for example, or to be drunk? What rules did this process conform to, or break? Is it OK to urinate in public? How far did it break the rules?

This small example demonstrates many of the differences that beset teams when they are solving problems (and also, incidentally, some of the issues that challenge the transfer of skills from the outdoors to the day job). Are there enough appropriate ideas, and do some of them break the paradigm – the way in which the problem has been set? Who decides what is an 'effective', as opposed to an 'efficient', answer to the problem? In an interesting (to say the least) debriefing, the tutor thought that the team had implemented their 'awful' ideas 'efficiently'.

This example also demonstrates the importance for team problem-solving of understanding the quality as well as the quantity of ideas and why it can be important to produce as many ideas as possible. It shows that unless teams have shared criteria they will struggle to come to an agreement about how best to solve their problems. It illustrates the difference between the 'Can we do it better?' and the 'Can we do it differently?' approaches. How acceptable is the solution in terms of group mores? This one was certainly challenging in terms of values. In certain societies it is considered not only acceptable but health-giving to drink your own urine, and urinating in public is also acceptable in some parts of the world. In many Muslim countries, such a suggestion would have been out of the question. Indeed, to have men and women problem-solving together would have been a non-starter in many cultures. So, the problem of transporting the water as described above relates to issues connected with problem-solving style, creative style, masculine and feminine approaches, values and national culture.

What was also interesting to us neutral onlookers as the scene was played out before us was that the proposer of the dramatic solution was quite oblivious to any of the possible constraints put forward by his peers. The only constraint he could see was one of time. Otherwise, he saw it as an efficient and effective answer to the problem. Would he have been able to convince the rest of the outdoors group if he had been a member of it? He certainly had a hard job on with the team he was now discussing it with. The degree of acceptance would have depended on the diversity dimensions that were present in the group, especially their problem-solving styles, creative styles, team role styles, values and national culture. If these are not known and understood in advance there will always be conflict. In this example there was no uncertainty concerning the problem before the group. They knew exactly what was expected of them. All they had to do was figure out a way to do it. It was not something that had never been done before, and had it been part of a work problem they could have consulted their colleagues and other sources of information to find an answer. Last but not the least of any leader's problems, how would you keep such an iconoclast happy in a team of conventional people, especially when such radical ideas might be necessary now and again for the team to solve its problems? Such a case study serves to illustrate some of the issues we feel are important in optimal team problem-solving, and emphasises how much more important these are in conditions of uncertainty.

The diversity factors

The following are the eight diversity factors which we believe can affect team performance:

1. *Problem-solving style.* All team members approach, define and solve problems using different styles.

2. *Creative style.* All team members are creative, but have different styles – they divide loosely into those who want to do things 'better' and those who want to do things 'differently'.

3. *Team role.* All team members have team roles, which fit

together (or not) to cover the team's work.

4.   *Values.* All team members have basic beliefs and reasons for doing things.

5.   *National culture.* All team members will behave in accordance with some aspects of their national culture.

6.   *Ethics.* All team members will have moral standards which they apply to business.

7.   *Masculine and feminine.* All team members have masculine or feminine approaches to their work (whatever their actual gender).

8.   *Technology.* All team members will have likes and dislikes in terms of how they communicate across distances and time frames.

Each of these factors is capable of preventing your team from performing well. Equally, each of them, when understood and used sensitively, can improve the performance of your team exponentially.

There may be other such factors, but our research has shown that the majority of people identify with these. They may have set you thinking about how particular factors have affected your team, or you may feel that you don't know enough about them at this stage to make a judgement. If the former, you might like to try Exercise 2 at the back of the book (page 229). This exercise is designed to help you to prioritise the different diversity variables for your team.

Psychometric questionnaires

We need to say a few words about the psychometric questionnaires that are mentioned and/or recommended in this book. Those we recommend are ones that we ourselves have used extensively. Most psychometrics require some kind of qualification or training on the part of the person carrying them out, before they can be administered. You are advised to check on what the requirement is in your own country, before embarking on a course of action. Usually it involves attending a training course run by the developer or licence holder of the psychometric in question. In some countries, such as the United States, there are stringent rules concerning who can access and administer these questionnaires.

You may personally have grave doubts about the efficacy of these types of questionnaire, but their predictive value is becoming more apparent as a number of long-term studies come to fruition. Research has been conducted for over a century to establish stable characteristics in populations and there is now considerable evidence that temperament is largely genetic. We have two views on these questionnaires. First of all, any questionnaire should represent the basis for discussion and not be seen as the last word on somebody's character. To this degree we believe that they can be very useful, especially in highlighting differences between individuals, which if unknown may lead to conflict. Secondly, they can be the basis for personal development. The mind should be seen as a muscle which can be trained and which can progressively improve if necessary.[7]

The words 'team' and 'group'

Another point we must make briefly at this stage is that most authors use the words 'team' and 'group' loosely and interchangeably. We feel strongly that a team has its own special characteristics, and throughout the book we give examples of where this is relevant. For the most part, however, we have tried to remain relaxed about the definition, in common with the authors we are quoting, as to do otherwise can become irritating to the reader. We have therefore generally referred to teams except when we are being specific about group characteristics or quoting from research.

Summary

What we have tried to do in this Introduction is to explain why we feel so strongly about the power of difference in teams and why we feel a book exploring the value and brilliance of diversity in teams is long overdue. We have introduced you to the model of Johari's Window in order to demonstrate the importance of trust and openness in a group and what happens when team members begin to trust one another. We believe this is important if problems are to be solved, especially where there is uncertainty. We have described a very small example of problem-solving and how it demonstrates how and where difference comes into play, and we have listed our diversity variables and given a short definition of each. In the second chapter, we go on to discuss the *raison d'être* of teams, look at problem-solving in more detail and explore what difference means in terms of your team.

What can you do about the power of diversity?

- Think about the level of trust and openness in your team. How much is there? Bear this in mind before you decide to try out any of the exercises with them. They might not be ready.

- What is the best team you have ever belonged to? Why do you think that was?

- Think about the composition of the different teams or groups, both inside and outside work, of which you have been a member. How did they vary in terms of how they approached problems? Was this because of any particular issue connected with diversity?

- Think about the times when your team has found it easy to solve a problem. Why do you think this was?

- Think about the times that your team has had difficulty in solving a problem. What do you think the reasons for this were?

- On your own, decide the order of importance for your team of the diversity variables (Exercise 1, page 227). Why do you think you have placed the variables in the order you have?

- Repeat this exercise with your team. Do all the members of the team agree? If not, what does this tell you?

Notes

[1] For a discussion of the difference between diversity and equal opportunities see www2.warwick.ac.uk/services/equalops/policies/diversity.

[2] ibid.

[3] Gardner, H. (2007) *Five Minds for the Future* (Boston, MA: Harvard Business School Press).

[4] Katzenbach, J. R. (1997) 'The myth of the top management team', *Harvard Business Review*, Nov.– Dec., pp. 83–91.

[5] Casey, D. (1985) 'When is a team not a team?', *Personnel Management*, Jan., pp. 26–9.

[6] This model was originated by Calvin Germain and his colleagues and has been developed within Deva.

[7] Try www.the-ba.net/personality for a quick personality test, or Nettle, D. (2007) *Personality: What Makes You the Way You Are* (Oxford: Oxford University Press).

2

On Teams, Problem-Solving and Diversity

What is a team and what are teams for?

Teams exist to solve a problem that cannot be solved by one person acting alone. That is their rationale. In fact, sometimes a team is used to solve a problem that would be better tackled by one person, but that is a different issue. There are a multitude of different ways in which teams can be put together depending on the problem they are there to solve.

Some teams are made up of people doing the same kind of work, grouped together conveniently under a leader who monitors their output. The problem here is to ensure that they all achieve the end result to the same standard in much the same way. An example of such a team might be an army platoon where everyone is an infantryman or a bombardier. Some teams are multi-disciplinary in nature, with individuals taking on different types of work required to achieve an end result. Sports teams would fall into this latter category, with individuals taking on specific roles such as goalkeeper or fly-half. Another example would be a project team, which is put together on a temporary basis to solve a problem which affects different areas of a business and needs representation from all its relevant parts. Yet other teams, and particularly those at the top of organisations, are made up of disciplines which together cover all the work required to run a business, such as finance director, operations director, procurement director and so on.

A further complication is added by defining the type of work teams do (i.e. what their output is). Some teams (e.g. a gang of labourers, or a team of stewards and stewardesses on a plane) may do physical work. Although they have to think for part of the time, most of what they do is carried out in actual working tasks. Some teams are able to combine thinking and doing, such as teams processing invoices. Some teams appear to do very little in the way of activity and appear to be only thinking. Nowadays many team members work from home. What difference does it make to team performance if one or more of your team members work all or part of the time from home? The problems associated with being able to think in a way that benefits the whole team are exacerbated if the team is a virtual one. A virtual team is where the members rarely come face to face with each other and communication may be by all sorts of electronic methods. We will be coming back to these issues under the heading 'The Power of Technology' in Chapter 10.

What all teams have in common is problem-solving. The basic function of a team is to problem-solve, bringing all their combined thinking and activities to bear on the issue in hand for the optimum result.

More heat than light has been shed on these different types of teams by management writers who argue for and against the necessity of 'real' team work, by which they mean that Holy Grail whereby the individuals in a team all have the same objective and work harmoniously to achieve it – what has been called 'a *small* number of people with *complementary skills* who are committed to a *common purpose, performance goals* and an *approach* for which they hold themselves *mutually accountable*.'[1] We will see later in this chapter one of the things that prevents this happening. What matters most to a team leader or member is the extent to which he or she needs to understand the differences in the team to bring the best available problem-solving talents to bear on the problem in hand.

Reg Revans was the first person to analyse the sort of work that teams were performing in terms of their thinking, because of his interest in action learning.[2] He pointed out that there is a difference between 'puzzles' and 'problems'. Puzzles are where there is a known answer to the issue, although it may not be known to the individual or group. A little more reading or asking the right questions of colleagues or experts will throw up the answer. They are an embarrassment to which a solution already exists – where there is a *right* answer. By contrast, 'problems' are those issues, challenges and opportunities where there is no single solution or one way of doing things. The solution might not even exist; different people in different circumstances will suggest different courses of action.

David Casey[3] developed a simple formula in order to give us some greater insights into team performance. He distinguished between co-operative groups and teams, and divided the work of these two groups into a similar taxonomy to that of Revans, but with an addition, coming up with simple puzzles, complex puzzles and problems. Casey believed that real teamwork requires so much effort, energy and persistence that he did not think it should be attempted unless there are very real problems to be solved – that is, where there is uncertainty surrounding the problem, and where people are prepared for the work involved in developing the required team behaviours. He produced two diagrams which clearly demonstrate what he had in mind.

Casey would say that the amount of information a team has to share to enable it to solve a problem has the most effect in categorising what sort of issue it is solving. In Figure 5 he shows that if there is *no need* to share, then the team is solving 'simple puzzles'. Not everyone would agree with us, but we would suggest that a football match is a simple puzzle. Although the amount of skill required to get the ball in the net is enormous, everyone knows what the aim is. There is no doubt as to where the goalposts are or in which direction the team should be pointing. Some people might say that there is so little sharing of the ball and so much prima donna behaviour on a football pitch that this is a good analogy, although others might say it properly belongs in the next category.

If there is *some need* to share then the team members need to co-operate as they are solving 'complex puzzles'. An example might be the crew of an ocean-going racing yacht, who have to share information on things such as navigational issues, weather conditions, strategy and tactics, but to whom a lot of things are also pretty obvious.

If it is *essential* for a team to share then they are solving problems. They have to pass through the sharing barrier and the uncertainty barrier, as it is likely that there is neither a shared understanding of the solution *nor* (and this is the most telling thing) a shared understanding of what the problem is in the first place. If you have found yourself agreeing or disagreeing about our definition of teams then you are beginning to think about this issue of the need to share, the emotional barriers to sharing, and the types of problems your own team has to face.

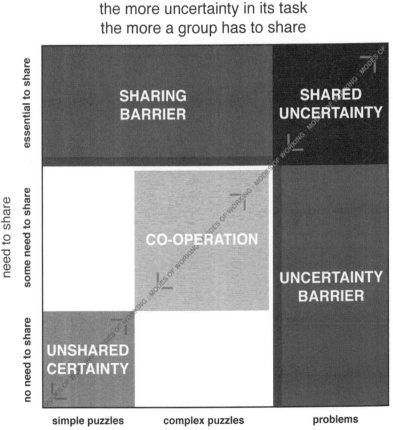

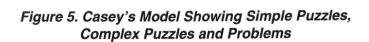

Figure 5. Casey's Model Showing Simple Puzzles,
Complex Puzzles and Problems

33

Having looked at this diagram you might want to decide where on the spectrum your team might be. It may be that your team does not need to share information – they are solving 'simple puzzles' – and it is your job as leader simply to apportion the tasks. In that case you may need to understand only a few of the diversities in your team, such as their problem-solving style and their team role. However, it is unlikely that you have picked up this book looking for solutions if that is the case. It may be that your team has some need to share and you are solving 'complex puzzles', in which case, some of the ideas in this book will help you to know where you need to put your energy in understanding the diversities in your team. Such knowledge will help you understand what is required to co-operate, negotiate and co-ordinate the work of the team, as you can see from Figure 6, which shows some feeling processes coming into play.

If as a team leader or team member you look at the diagram and realise that your team is solving 'problems' where it is essential to share information, then you need to take a good look at Figure 6. Such a team requires the highest degree of interpersonal skills because task processes and feelings processes are equal, and your team has to be capable of moving through the Uncertainty and Sharing Barriers *and* the Feelings Barrier.

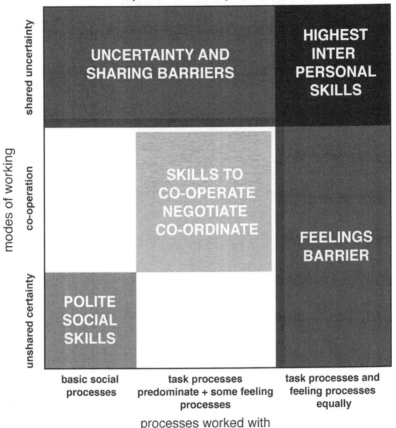

Figure 6. Casey's model showing the type of skills needed for different situations

As business life gets more complex and every team starts to face issues they have not faced before, particularly concerning change and continuous improvement, it is likely that more and more teams will have to look at what it is they have to share and what this involves, and realise that they are solving 'problems', at least some of the time (see Exercise 3, page 230).

Another way of looking at this issue might be to look at the lists of behaviours that Casey drew up to distinguish between Co-operative Groups and Teams. Bear in mind that he considered that Co-operative Groups solve simple and complex puzzles and that Teams solve problems. It is Teams, even if they only solve problems some of the time, that are likely to need to be particularly aware of all their diversity factors or variables if they are to be as successful as they could be.

In a Co-operative Group, according to Casey:

- People work together.
- Commitment is high.
- Process issues are worked on covertly.
- People negotiate with each other.
- Information is passed on a 'need to know' basis.
- Conflict is accommodated.
- Politics are important.
- Feelings are not part of the work.
- Trust and openness are measured.
- Difficult decisions may be by compromise.[4]

In a Team:

- People trust each other's judgement and behaviour.
- Feelings are expressed freely.
- Process issues are part of the work.
- Commitment is high.
- Objectives are common to all, and everyone knows them.
- Listening is high.
- Conflict is worked through; the task is stopped where necessary.
- Decisions are by consensus.[5]

Although a few things are common to both sets of descriptions, it is only in the second list that conflict is worked through and decisions are by consensus. It is not a question of commitment (that is high in both), but in teams that solve problems people *trust* each other's judgement and behaviour – a point we will come back to later in this chapter. Try Exercise 4 (page 231) to determine where you and your team are.

Other researchers have made similar findings. One study shows that while organisations use 'team' and 'group' interchangeably there are differences between them.[6] Its authors suggest that teams create resources and add to their environments while groups manage and redistribute their resources, and further that teams have stable, valued interpersonal relations and groups do not. If you want to be a team that creates resources and adds to its environment then you need to have understood all the diversity factors in your team. Try discussing this issue with your team/group. What do they think?

Working with newly formed teams in the reorganised National Health Service we discovered that one of their biggest problems was finding the time to discuss all the issues pertinent to them as a team at their weekly meeting. Sometimes they were all involved and sometimes different members of the team were involved. It was difficult to know what category any subject was in until they started to discuss it. This was at a time when these teams were feeling their way and nearly everything they discussed required a new policy, often affecting many members of the team. They found the idea of whether an issue was in the top right part of Casey's model or in the middle part a very helpful litmus test of how many people, and who, should get involved. Thus they were able to schedule meetings of the requisite numbers of people outside their weekly meeting and just report the outcomes, or else discuss the issue as a team. Our experience has been borne out by (unpublished) research on a highly successful airline in Australia. Although there was no need for the management team to demonstrate team-like behaviour or high integration around many issues, the trick was to recognise those where this was necessary – and work accordingly.

We now go on to look at problem-solving in more detail in order to understand its vital importance for team performance.

What is problem-solving?

It is rather sobering to think that the study of problem-solving originated in the field of learning theory and was primarily laboratory-based. Researchers like Pavlov[7] (dogs) and Skinner[8] (rats) examined the conditions under which and the mechanisms by which particular stimuli and particular responses became connected. When attention turned from animals to humans, Gagné[9] developed a hierarchy of learning, with classical conditioning (i.e. the behaviour identified by Pavlov and Skinner) at the bottom and problem-solving at the pinnacle, representing the highest, most complex form of learning. He said that it involved recombining two or more principles into new ones, making it possible to answer questions and solve problems. Learning and problem-solving went hand in hand. Language was critical in a sharing of, and an understanding of, the problem to be solved by individuals in a group, as everyone would have their own concept of what the problem might be that needed to be solved.

According to Dr Michael Kirton, a leading theorist in this field, individuals differ in terms of how they approach, define and solve problems, but this diversity in teams is essential if all problems are to be solved.[10] There is a view, he says, that the whole of problem-solving is based on the different ways in which people use structure. We will be looking at this and some other findings of Kirton's in more detail in the following chapter on problem-solving. Another writer, David Jonassen,[11] has developed a whole taxonomy of problems, including what he calls 'well-structured problems' and 'ill-structured problems, which possess multiple solutions, solution paths, or no solutions at all'. His research showed that 'communication patterns in teams differed when solving well-structured and ill-structured problems'. He also felt that the more complex a problem the more difficult it would be for one person to possess all the abilities needed for solving it, thereby indicating the need for diversity in problem-solving. Research shows that people rush into solving a problem without sharing with one another what they think the problem is really about or without appreciating that their suggested solution may throw up all sorts of other problems[12]. This leads to all sorts of difficulties and ensures that teams are not always as productive as they might be.

So far, we hope that we have demonstrated that understanding the type of problem you are addressing is very important in terms of how successful your team might be. But there are lots of other issues involved before you can get all your team members aligned for solving the problem in hand. Perhaps this is a good time to stop and ask the questions we posed in the Introduction: 'Why do I have to use my energy to get my team to work together? Why do individuals in teams not work together more harmoniously and produce better results?' – an issue that was also raised by Casey in his team lists above, where he states that in a 'real' team members trust each other.

Why do teams not work together better?

We would be surprised if, as the leader of a team, you have not asked yourself this question with a great sigh. Why can't they just get on with each other and get on with the job at the same time? It would make life so much easier. Even as a team member you may be tired of the perpetual politics engaged in by your team and wish people would spend as much energy on the task as they do on jockeying for position.

One management writer, David Nadler, sums up these views when he says:

> The quality of interpersonal relationships among group members often leaves much to be desired. People fall too readily into patterns of competitiveness, conflict and hostility; only rarely do a group's members support and help one another as difficult ideas and issues are worked through.[13]

It is a sad reflection on how little satisfaction people appear to receive from teams at work that a trainer at Team Management Systems (TMS) Development International Ltd in York told us that, when asked about their best experience in a team, most people will give an answer from outside work, relating to voluntary work or a hobby. Whether this satisfaction is a function of the shared values that people hold in teams that come together voluntarily is something we will examine later under 'Values' and 'Ethics'. Or is it simply that there is too much conflict at work and people do not trust each other?

The reason people behave badly when working together is that in every individual there are conflicting needs for independence and socialisation.[14] These needs, and how they are reconciled, differ from person to person, so that two people in the same situation will behave differently depending on those needs. However, the way these two polarised needs present themselves to the individual also depends on the amount of resources available to be shared, and in a team all sorts of resources are rationed – pay, bonuses, the regard and attention of the manager, etc. What this means in practice is that individuals want their own way in things as often as they possibly can, without forfeiting the goodwill of their friends and colleagues. Internally, they are thinking that their ideas are the best ones, their views the right ones, their course of action the only one that will fit the bill. Because people are diverse in all the ways that we will come to discuss, everyone is thinking in this individualistic way, with different ideas, views and corresponding actions. However, most people also want to be given the love and affection they think is theirs by right. In teams we probably would not think of using these words, but would speak rather in terms of recognition – of people obtaining a hearing for their ideas, an opportunity to speak, a share of the spoils, etc. Often, the only way for an individual to manage this dichotomy is by negotiating down from having everything their own way to a position of give-and-take – where they accord others in the team at least some of the same recognition that they want for themselves. An example would be of a manager negotiating a budget for his team. The team members rely on him or her to do well for them, but the manager is also competing with others in the same peer group and has also to satisfy his or her superiors. In conditions of uncertainty these anxieties about the amount of resources available is likely to increase, and this exacerbates these diametrically opposed needs and provokes team members to new heights of conflict and disruptive behaviour. Recently, the President of the United States, George Bush, was reported as saying he wants to be loved. Even though he looks in the mirror and tells himself that he did the right thing – he did it his way.[15]

We were reminded forcibly of this conflict recently when a neighbour's child aged twelve went off on a weekend camping trip organised by her school. Each group of fourteen children was given a sum of money with which to buy several meals, supervised by an external group leader. Her group contained a member with coeliac disease (an allergy to gluten). With the team having worked everything out to the last crust of bread to be bought, the member with the allergy decided she wanted to eat bread too, even though it was bad for her, which meant that another girl went without. Another of the girls used the surplus money that existed, not to buy the sweets that had been agreed upon, but a copy of *Heat* magazine, and then wouldn't allow anyone else to read it, thereby demonstrating the power of advertising as that is exactly what the magazine's advert suggests. Finally, two girls were left to do the washing up for the fourteen. Typical selfish behaviour from girls of this age, you might think. What surprised us was not so much the behaviour of the girls, who didn't know any better, but the inadequacies of the group leader. Rather than carrying out a debriefing to discuss what had happened, the effects on others and the lessons to be learnt, he seemed to some observers to be too busy fraternising with some of the teachers! This sort of sloppily supervised group dynamics is all too common and is very damaging. Those who behaved well on this occasion may now be full of resentment and may not behave so well next time. Those who behaved badly have got away with it this time, but on another occasion, when it matters more, they may find that they are thwarted. On this occasion they were not challenged and apparently did not lose any goodwill. But resentment may be smouldering under the surface. What are these occasions with group leaders for if not to discuss and explain behaviour?

These competing claims are particularly observable when a new group or team get together. They are well summed up in the theories of Tuckman and Jensen,[16] who developed a model for group development with two sets of variables which they described as 'personal relations' and 'task functions'. Groups, by working through dependency, tension, cohesion and interdependence in the former, and orientation, organisation, open data flow and problem-solving in the latter, arrive at 'Form, Storm, Norm, and Perform'. This means that new teams initially spend time, often noisily, debating issues, and not getting very far until they develop 'norms' (i.e. methods of working). Often, teams that regularly work together have found a way of working so that when they meet there is less and less storming time. However, this storming time is an essential part of the process and has to be catered for whenever groups first get together to achieve a task. In fact, the 'storming' part may take much longer than the actual performing. We have formed the habit of conducting an exercise at the beginning of our seminars which uses the storming of groups to good effect. It is very important to give people the opportunity for letting off steam as early as possible by stating their grievances and having a say – rather like having a running-round game before a story at children's parties.

The competing claims of individuality and affiliation are particularly evident when a team is malfunctioning and team members can see that things are going wrong. In these circumstances how are individuals to regain the trust of their fellow team members? If people are to work together over a sustained period they need to be able to predict what the likely behaviour of the other individuals in their problem-solving group might be. Understanding the application of the diversity variables which comprise the main part of this book is a way of doing this. Any theories or instruments which would explain these differences would also be helpful. During the course of describing the diversity variables we will suggest any such instruments or questionnaires that we think might be helpful. Some are available at little expense, but others require considerable expertise and a course of study – a small price to pay for all the research that has gone into them and the dividends they pay. Many of these instruments help to create a shared language which enables team members to understand the diversity within the team and to discuss their differences in an objective and intelligent way. As Peter Senge has said, a shared language is absolutely crucial in enabling groups to work together (see below).[17]

The behaviour of all individuals is fuelled by anxiety. This anxiety has multiple sources, but there are also anxieties associated with being in a team which manifest as questions: 'How will I measure up?', 'What if I can't make a contribution?', etc. The American psychoanalyst Glen Gabbard hypothesised a hierarchy of anxiety which begins with the most primitive level of disintegration anxiety (the anxiety connected with being annihilated or losing one's sense of identity) and goes up to super-ego anxiety (being in conflict with one's own set of values).[18] Karen Horney emphasised the intensity and ubiquity of anxiety.[19] She believed, for example, that workaholism in individuals is an attempt to control intense anxiety. One of her important contributions was to realise the need to grapple with one's hostile influences while maintaining one's connection to others. Clearly this comes acutely into focus in the intimate team situation. We believe that this anxiety can be reduced if people have a deeper understanding of their fellow team members and are able to discuss differences using a neutral language. For example, in Chapter 4, 'The Power of Creativity', we boldly state that everyone is creative, but has a different style of manifesting it. We have found that, in many teams, there is concern about 'creativity'. Many people feel that they are labelled as 'not creative' and as a result feel that their contribution is either not valued or is undervalued. By explaining the diversity of creative styles we are able to put some of these fears to rest. This understanding leads to the development of a language with which to internalise difference, as discussed below.

The importance of shared language

In *The Fifth Discipline*, Senge writes about creating dialogue, and about the sharing of mental models and assumptions among team members.[20] Dialogue is about talking things over so that the best idea is adopted rather than someone winning the argument. The result is a free exploration that brings to the surface the full depth of people's experience and thought. Senge follows up the work of a leading quantum theorist[21] in suggesting that dialogue occurs when a group becomes open to the flow of a larger intelligence. The most important thing is to break down the linear mental models which each member of a team brings to the problem-solving situation. But how can understanding the diversity that individuals bring to this mix help? Won't it just complicate things further? Let's pause here and look at the role of diversity in other aspects of our life.

What has diversity ever done for us?

It comes as something of a shock to realise that the Japanese word for 'different', '*chigau*', also means 'wrong'.[22] It is quite simple. In Japan if you think differently from the other members of your group you must be wrong. While this may be comforting when gaining consensus is the goal, it also indicates the possibility of the lowest common denominator. Senge[23] defines a 'focusing down' type of consensus that seeks the common denominator in multiple and individual views, and an 'opening up' type of consensus, that seeks a picture larger than any one person's point of view. It is a moot point, addressed by all problem-solvers at some stage, whether or not the solution that is acceptable to most people is the best solution. There are clearly many problems where this acceptability criterion would not be the key to the best solution. You may have come across them yourself as a team leader, when your role has been to lead your team to implement what was the best solution, not perhaps to do what was acceptable, or where the consensus was of the 'focusing down' type.

When people talk about diversity, especially in the workplace, they usually mean differences of race, gender, religious adherence and, more recently, age, and indeed these are important because each of them will result in a different point of view. In fact, the British government has actually identified six areas of diversity – race, age, gender, sexual orientation, disability and religious belief – and set up a Commission for Equalities and Human Rights to ensure that there is a central focus for these, besides having named 2007 The Year of Diversity. There is also a National Centre for Diversity, an independent body which aims to help employers share best practice. As Erika Lucas suggests in *Making Inclusivity a Reality*,[24] perhaps the best place to start is with an agreed definition of what diversity is. Guidance from the Chartered Management Institute[25] suggests it is about 'valuing the differences between people and the ways in which these differences can contribute to a richer, more creative and more productive environment', a sentiment with which we would agree even though we have widened the list of variables, beyond that usually seen as the norm.

A Chartered Institute of Personnel and Development electronic survey conducted in early 2006 provided valuable benchmarking information on the state of play in UK organisations regarding diversity progress generally and what drives that change.[26] It showed that the top driver for progress is law, although many of the employers failed to address the full range of statutory discrimination provisions. Business drivers for change included recruiting the best talent, improvements in customer relations, creativity and performance. It said that most employers fail to grasp the full nature of the business case, which suggests that there is huge potential for adding value to business performance if organisations get smarter at managing diversity. We would agree with this, and in writing this book have attempted both to widen and to focus the debate. We discuss many more aspects of diversity than hitherto and focus specifically on the work of teams and what can be done to release their specific potential.

Coca-Cola in America has widened what it considers to be the attributes of a diverse workforce considerably. These include:

- Skills and abilities
- Education
- Race
- Religion
- Nationality
- Sexual orientation
- Gender
- Family status
- Position
- Personality
- Skill mix
- Job experience
- Learning styles
- Thinking styles

Coca-Cola also maintains that there are four generations of people in the workforce, each with their own profile. They are the Matures, the Baby Boomers, Generation X and the Millennials (Generation Y). They are classified according to: dates they were born, 'Formative Events', experience 'In the Workplace' and applicable 'Coaching Tips'.

As Michael Kirton has explained[27] the sort of diversity that a group contains can be likened to the diversity of bacteria contained in the human body. Humans each contain about one kilogram of bacteria, a few potentially hostile, a few friendly and the rest neutral, but a pool of potential resource. We have more DNA than we need.[28] In that surplus diversity is the key to success in constantly developing to survive, for example in combating hostile micro-organisms that are themselves in constant development. The lesson from nature seems to be that neutral diversity, as long as it is only modestly expensive to keep, is well worth tolerating by the host as a potential pool from which change can emerge if the need arises. Work with fruit flies has indicated that something different in an individual fly – for example rare characteristics in males – creates more success in mating.[29] This is also true of rare trees or animals – they tend to be able to fend off predators and disease – until they become common. Nature appears to point to the conclusion that genetic diversity represents a critical pool of opportunity for change, which is vital to survival. W. Ross Ashby has shown that in cybernetics there is a law of 'requisite variety'.[30] The more attributes any issue possesses, the more these need to be matched. Danny Miller has pointed out that organisations which have this 'requisite variety' can adapt to the changes in their environment.[31] Why has no one thought of applying this idea systematically to teams? For a *logical* explanation of why diversity can be better than ability we recommend Scott E. Page's book, *The Difference*.[32]

Diversity and change

As Michael Kirton has indicated, an individual's management of diversity begins with the brain.[33] As we have made our world more complex and become more dependent on collaboration with other problem-solvers, we have learned to differentiate between 'us' and 'them'. The former are categorised as being same, safe and therefore useful, whereas the latter seem to be less similar and possibly less safe – perhaps then not useful but hostile. Many organisms have instincts to help them in this problem-solving, but to humans it is yet another problem to solve. We need to understand better the trade-off between the obvious economy of effort that comes with dealing with limited diversity, with people who are like us (sometimes called 'similarity attraction'), and the immediate or potential value of accommodating wider diversity. Diversity creates complexity, which in turn presents challenges for all individuals and creates resentments within those with limited capacity for complexity. A narrowly diverse team can exist in steady state for some considerable time. However, given the world's current rapidity of change it is more likely that such a team will collapse and a more diverse team be needed. A wide range of problems requires a wide range of problem-solvers, who in turn are difficult to manage. Kirton has written:

> Groups form to solve Problem A. By doing so we have acquired Problem B – how to manage each other. Unsuccessful problem-solving teams spend more energy on Problem B rather than on Problem A.[34]

In summary, then, it would appear that we do not bring the diversities of a team into play sufficiently, partly because we do not know what they are and partly because we cannot handle complexity. There are other reasons – for instance, we do not recognise the problem that needs the diversities and we do not invest time in them even when we do. Casey is right. If the prize is great enough we cannot invest enough, but we have to know that it is.

Does diversity work?

There is evidence that diversity (even in its narrow definition) can improve problem-solving. One of the most comprehensive articles in the literature, by Cox and Blake,[35] brings together much of the research on managing diversity and organisational competitiveness in American companies. Among several areas which the authors think benefit from heterogeneity (mostly in culture and gender) are creativity and problem-solving. They cite Rosbeth Moss Kanter,[36] whose study of innovation in organisations as far back as 1983 revealed that the most innovative companies deliberately established heterogeneous teams to 'create a marketplace of ideas, recognising that a multiplicity of points of view need to be brought to bear on a problem'. Kanter also noted that organisations strong on innovation had done a better job than most in eradicating racism, sexism and classism. Research by Charlene Nemeth concluded that groups exposed to minority views were more creative than more homogeneous groups.[37] She further concluded that persistent exposure to minority viewpoints stimulates creative thought processes. Cox and Blake point out that the same is true of problem-solving:

> Diverse groups have a broader and richer base of experience from which to approach a problem. Thus managing diversity also has the potential to improve problem-solving and decision-making[38].

They conclude:

> In sum, culturally diverse workforces create competitive advantage through better decisions. A variety of perspectives brought to the issue, higher levels of critical analysis of alternatives through minority influence effects, and lower probability of groupthink, all contribute.'[39]

They do have caveats. They believe that the support of top management and training in cultural awareness are critical to success. The Chartered Management Institute agrees with this. In its Guidance for Managers, *The Growing Importance of Diversity in the Workplace*, it points out not only the legal case but the business case too.[40] It believes that a diverse workforce brings benefits in the areas of recruitment and retention, improved morale and job satisfaction, leading to greater productivity and access to untapped markets. If this is true of workforces, it must also be true of teams.

We have a concern that, in emphasising the differences between people rather than their similarities, we might be labelled divisive. Perhaps our position is best summed up by Tsvetan Todorov in his book *On Human Diversity*.[41] In describing Montesquieu's various writings on the topic of cultural difference he said that he conceptualised 'the diversity of peoples and the unity of the human race at one and the same time'. We would like to think that we have explored the diversity of individuals in teams while at the same time assuming that these individuals have shared objectives in terms of what is best for the team.

Summary

In this chapter we have looked at what teams are there to do and the many ways in which they can undertake their tasks. We have described the difference between Co-operative Groups and Teams and what makes them different, and have given you some ideas about how you can distinguish between them for yourself. It is important that you decide what you want your team to be able to achieve and are realistic about it. We have also tried to explain why people seem to behave the way they do when they work together and how such behaviour can best be ameliorated. We have shown how difference works for and against us in other aspects of life, and how important it is to harness diversity and make it work for you in your team.

We have already listed the diversity factors, as we see them, in the Introduction. The rest of the book describes each factor in more detail, explains why it is important, and shows how you, as either team leader or team member, can use it to improve your team performance and make your team more effective. We give an example of a psychometric that might help you to understand the make-up of your team in terms of many of the diversities, and also examples of what we have found works and, in some instances, what doesn't.

We now start, in the next chapter, with perhaps the biggest difference of all between humans – our problem-solving style.

What can you do about teams, problem-solving and diversity?

- You can work through the Casey model with your team in terms of whether the team is an Uncooperative Group, a Co-operative Group or a Team – see Exercise 3 (page 230).

- You can work through the Casey model with your team and do Exercise 4 on Categories (page 231). How much of your work falls into the categories of 'simple puzzles', 'complex puzzles' and 'problems' and what are the implications for your team?

- You can talk over Fisher's work with your team and decide if under his categories you are a group or a team. Does this match the Casey model?

- How does your team work through the Tuckman and Jensen model? Do you allow storming time? Does your team do nothing *but* storm? What is stopping your team from 'norming'?

- Does your team concentrate on the 'focusing down' type of consensus that seeks the common denominator, or the 'opening up' type that seeks a picture larger than any one person's point of view? Which would be the most effective for you?

- Does your team listen to minority voices? How do you know what diversity you have? Have you audited it?

- Have you thought of introducing diversity into your team by including members of other teams, suppliers, customers, etc.?

Notes

[1] Katzenbach, J. R. (1997) 'The myth of the top management team', *Harvard Business Review*, Nov.– Dec., pp. 83–91.

[2] Revans, R. (1980) *Action Learning: New Techniques for Management* (London: Blond & Briggs).

[3] Casey, D. (1985) 'When is a team not a team?', *Personnel Management*, Jan., pp. 26–9.

[4] ibid.

[5] ibid.

[6] Fisher, S. G., Hunter, T. A. and Macrossan, W. D. K. (1997) 'Team or group? Managers' perception of the difference', *Journal of Managerial Psychology*, vol. 12, issue 4.

[7] Pavlov, I. P. (trans. G. V. Anrep) (1927) *Conditioned Reflexes: An Investigation of the Physiological Activity of the Cerebral Cortex* (London: Oxford Univbersity Press).

[8] Skinner, B. F. (1973) *Beyond Freedom and Dignity* (New York: Knopf).

[9] Gagné, R. M. (1974) 'Problem Solving and Thinking', *Annual Review of Psychology*, 10.

[10] Kirton, M. J. (ed.) (1994) *Adaptors and Innovators: Styles of Creativity and Problem-solving* (London: Routledge), rev. pbk edn.

[11] Jonassen, D. H. (2000) 'Toward a Design Theory of Problem Solving', *Educational Technology Research and Development*, vol. 48, no. 4, Dec. (Boston, MA: Springer).

[12] Kirton, M. J. (ed.) (1994) *Adaptors and Innovators: Styles of Creativity and Problem-solving* (London: Routledge), rev. pbk edn.

[13] Nadler, D., Hackman, J. and Lawlor, E. (1979) *Managing Organisational Behaviour* (Boston, MA: Little, Brown).

[14] van der Molen, P. P. (1994 [1989]) 'Adaption-Innovation and changes in social structure: on the anatomy of catastrophe', in Kirton, *Adaptors and Innovators*.

[15] President George Bush, televised interview, 12 July 2007.

[16] Tuckman, B. W. and Jensen, M. A. (1977) 'Stages of small group development revisited', *Group and Organisational Studies*, 2.

[17] Senge, P. (1993 [1990]) *The Fifth Discipline: The Art and Practice of the Learning Organisation* (London: Century).

[18] Quoted in Kreps, J. I. (2006) 'Anxiety', *Islamica*, 18.

[19] Horney, K. (1946) *Our Inner Conflicts: A Constructive Theory of Neurosis* (London: Routledge).

[20] Senge, P. (1993 [1990]) *The Fifth Discipline: The Art and Practice of the Learning Organisation* (London: Century).

[21] Bohm, D. (1965) *The Special Theory of Relativity* (New York: Benjamin).

[22] Taken from a review by Harriet Sergeant of *The Blue-eyed Salaryman*, by Niall Murtagh (2005), *The Spectator*, 2 Apr. 2005.

[23] Senge, P. (1993 [1990]) *The Fifth Discipline: The Art and Practice of the Learning Organisation* (London: Century).

[24] Lucas, E. (2007) 'Making inclusivity a reality', *Professional Manager*, vol. 16, issue 4, Jul.

[25] Chartered Management Institute (2006) *Guidance for Managers: The Growing Importance of Diversity in the Workplace*.

[26] Worman, D. (2006) 'Managing diversity is the business', *Impact: Quarterly Update on CIPD Policy and Research*, issue 17(1), Oct.

[27] Kirton, M. J. (2003) *Adaption-Innovation: In the Context of Diversity and Change* (London: Routledge).

[28] Jones, S. (2000) The Language of the Genes (London: Flamingo), 2nd rev. edn.

[29] Petite, C. (1958) 'Le determinisme genetique et psycho-phisiologique de la competition sexuelle chez drosophila elangaster', *Bulletin Biologique*, vol. 92, pp. 248–329.

[30] Ashby, W. R. (1956) *Introduction to Cybernetics* (New York: Wiley).

[31] Miller, D. (1990) *The Icarus Paradox: How Exceptional Companies Bring About Their Own Downfall* (London: HarperCollins).

[32] Page, Scott, E., (2007), *The Difference: How the power of diversity creates better groups, firms, schools, and societies*, (New Jersey: Princeton University Press).

[33] Kirton, M. J. (2003) *Adaption-Innovation: In the Context of Diversity and Change* (London: Routledge).

[34] Kirton, M. J. (ed.) (1994) *Adaptors and Innovators: Styles of Creativity and Problem-solving* (London: Routledge), rev. pbk edn.

[35] Cox, T. H. and Blake, S. (1991) 'Managing cultural diversity: implications for organisational competitiveness', *Academy of Management Executive*, vol. 5, no. 3, p. 45.

[36] Kanter, R. M. (1983) *The Change Masters* (New York: Simon & Schuster).

[37] Nemeth, C. J. (1986) 'Differential contributions of majority and minority influence', *Psychological Review*, vol. 93, pp. 23–32.

[38] Cox, T. H. and Blake, S. (1991) 'Managing cultural diversity: implications for organisational competitiveness', *Academy of Management Executive*, vol. 5, no. 3, p.

[39] ibid.

[40] Chartered Management Institute, *Guidance for Managers*.

[41] Todorov, T. (trans. C. Porter) (1993) *On Human Diversity, Nationalism, Racism, and Exoticism in French Thought* (London: Harvard University Press).

3

The Power of Problem-Solving Style

Introduction

This chapter is about the power of problem-solving style. It is based on two premises. The first is that teams exist to solve problems great and small – that is their *raison d'être*. The second is that everyone has a different approach to solving problems, no matter what the problem might be, i.e. their problem-solving style. This difference is what they bring to the team situation. What follows is not concerned with different types of objective problem-solving *models*, such as algorithms, or binary decision-making processes. What this chapter does is describe the different problem-solving *styles* that individuals have and how they approach, define and solve problems. It demonstrates how powerful it can be when individuals understand not only their own style of solving problems, but also those of other people, and apply those styles appropriately and effectively. In this chapter we discuss different theories of cognition (how you think) and give some practical examples of why this is probably the most important diversity a team can get to grips with. In order to differentiate between this cognitive approach and other methods the team might use to solve problems (e.g the different knowledge and skills in the group), we have used the words 'problem-solving style' wherever appropriate.

Matters of perception

One of the biggest conflict-engendering issues to affect teams is that of not understanding why one of your colleagues has a particular viewpoint or approach. Their approach simply may not make sense to you at all. And what is worse you have no language or framework with which to begin to discuss your differences. You cannot have a discussion about it, because you do not know where to start. You cannot articulate it. Whether they are aware of it or not, this is what is happening in most teams which blithely start problem-solving. And, not surprisingly, this results in a lot of misunderstanding and poor solutions. Over time you may get used to someone's habitual approach, but it still irritates because it is so different from your own. If you understood how useful having a range of styles could be in the team, and how they could be applied, you would be able to solve a far wider range of problems – and more amicably!

Let us give a very small example of seeing things from a different point of view. After thirty years of knowing each other, the authors discovered quite by chance that they each had a completely different idea of what a 'family butcher' was. One of us thought that it meant the business belonged to a family, perhaps father and son, or daughter. The other thought it meant that they supplied meat to families (as opposed to anyone else). A quick straw poll of friends demonstrated that everyone had a slightly different idea: 'knows you personally', 'not a national chain', 'sources locally', 'wears a white coat'. Turning to Google, we discovered that the term had been current since the fifteenth century, but this didn't make the meaning any clearer. Now, if we had been setting out to solve some problem associated with family butchers and this rather basic dichotomy had not surfaced, we would immediately have started on solving the problem from opposite ends of the spectrum. Now in the great scheme of things it hardly matters that we have this different point of view, but in business situations it might matter a great deal. You only have to have this happen a few times – for example, one person to be thinking Metric and the other Imperial – for chaos to ensue. (This is not as silly as it sounds; problems with grinding the mirror of the Hubble telescope were caused by just such a difference.[1]) We go into these differences and their effects in more detail under the paragraphs on 'mindset' below.

From our research we know that, when asked, most members of teams would say that one of the reasons a team was effective was that the members' problem-solving style was known and understood and was used to good effect. In the ineffective teams the reverse was true – it was not known and it was not used. Many people who did not know it felt that it would have been useful to know. When asked to rank the diversity variables in order of their importance for an effective team, they always saw problem-solving style as the most important. But of course, we do not know what our respondents were thinking about when they gave an opinion on problem-solving style (even though we gave them a definition). They may all have had a different view of it!

In the text below we start to unravel some of the issues relating to cognitive/problem-solving style and its effects. We describe various methods of determining this style and we discuss some examples that we have experienced. Before we do this, however, we want to make a small digression to talk about 'mindset' and its relevance to problem-solving.

Mindset

'Mindset' means 'a fixed and predominant way of thinking and seeing'.[2] This means that no two people 'see' the world in exactly the same way. We are using 'see' here in a metaphorical way as we take in information from all our senses, but seeing is the sense that we use the most. Perhaps 'perception' would be a better word to use, but it has a rather superior ring to it! This disparity between people should be thought of as an issue rather than as a problem, because the very fact that people see things differently is both an asset and a problem. It is an asset because it means that we can solve a whole range of problems, but it is a problem because it means that coming to an agreement about what the problem actually is, never mind getting to solve it, can take some time.

Let's explore a couple of examples of seeing in action. We come from a place which according to the older style of number plates was designated as BU. As small children we spent hours in the back of our parents' car amusing ourselves by looking for number plates, and there was special joy if, miles from home, we spotted the BU. Now, driving anywhere in Britain we do not have to be looking for this number plate for it simply to leap out at us from the passing traffic. In fact, there are so many that we think it may be the registration of a hire car company. This is an example of 'selective seeing' – where, because our minds have been alerted to something, we tend to pick it up without any difficulty. You may have noticed this when you have bought, or are thinking about buying, a new car. Suddenly the car you have in mind, or have just purchased, seems to be everywhere. Is it really? No. You have given your mind a template to work on and it has done its job. Incidentally, this is how you can scan reading material very easily and quickly if you know the words you are looking for. Another example, using another sense, would be a mother hearing her baby crying when no one else does. She is on the alert for the sound.

If you take this example to its logical conclusion it means that we filter out information that we do not think is relevant in place of information that we think is. This filter uses our 'grid of experience' (Figure 7). Our 'grid' makes a match in some way with incoming information.

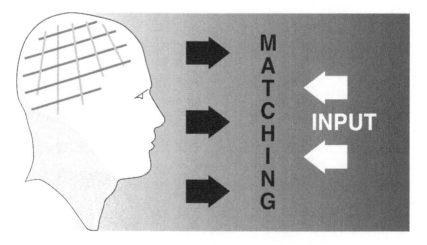

Figure 7. The grid of experience

56

'Selective seeing' is a mechanism that we have been refining from childhood through nature and nurture, and in the main it serves us very well. Just imagine what would happen if you had to test everything before you got out of bed in the morning and could not take anything for granted. How do you know that when you place your foot on the floor beside the bed you will not be putting it into a sea of acid? How do you know that there isn't a poisonous creature in your slippers? (In some parts of the world, of course, that is quite likely and you would check for this.) How do you know that there isn't itching powder in your dressing-gown? How do you know that the water is safe to clean your teeth in? Now you may think that this is very silly. However, it is a way of making you think about all the things you *don't* usually think about, in order to demonstrate that you habitually filter out a great deal of information. We are so busy scanning, testing, rejecting and selecting information that we are not even aware that we are doing it. If you had dropped a glass on your hard bedroom floor you would be wary about padding about in bare feet. We make assumptions on the basis of past experience, expectations and knowledge.

Take the picture in Figure 8 (overleaf). What can you see? Has your mind already made a match with this image or are you completely open as to what it might be?

Figure 8. What can you see?

On one of our courses for a shipbuilding company we had moved on from this slide when a voice suddenly said, 'I know what it is now – it's a Type-22 frigate.' He was referring to that tiny blob in the bottom middle of the picture. His whole vision was focused on selecting that tiny piece of the picture and ignoring the rest.

What do you think the whole picture is? Of course, in certain circumstances whatever you think it is is what it is. That is your reality. However, there is perhaps an image contained in the picture that many people could agree upon.

Yes, it's a cow. Can you see it now? Does having an image of a cow in your mind help you? It is not an ordinary cow. It is a white cow with no legs. The cow's body is in profile but its head is turned towards you with two prominent ears and a mouth. Have you

58

matched it now? Do not worry if you cannot match the cow. You may have a grid that is relatively free from this image. Even when we were working with an organisation founded on products from the cow, many people could not see it. The cow is an old idea, which nearly all cultures have in their grid. If it cannot be seen, imagine how difficult it is to see a new idea.

This is also the mechanism whereby organisations mould the minds of their employees into a unified whole and develop a culture. Most people will feel uncomfortable if they cannot see the cow, because they want to have their own experience, but once you have seen the cow it is quite difficult to 'unsee' it. A mindset has been created. Whenever you introduce a new idea to a team this process of matching and mismatching will take place. Some of the team will understand it and some will not. Sometimes we have to be very explicit when we are sharing information with each other and check assumptions. 'This is my version of reality – it looks like this.' The same process is going on in relation to any problem that we are faced with. We spontaneously start to go through the grid process when we try to find an answer. But each of us rejects and selects quite different material to come to our conclusions. So perception is a double-edged sword and we have to know how to wield it to best effect.

If you have a practising Buddhist on your team these ideas will be very familiar to them, as they form the basis of much of the Buddha's teaching. Buddhists believe that there is no absolute reality and that we mustn't rely on our senses, as they are unique to individuals. They call this *'sunyata'*, which roughly translated from the Sanskrit means 'emptiness' or 'voidness'. It does not mean that Buddhists approach problems without emotion or compassion – far from it – but that they are more aware that everything is interdependent. It is a pity that we cannot adopt this way of looking at things when we approach a problem, instead of bringing a huge agenda of thoughts and feelings to it. Of course, the fact that Buddhists have this view does not mean that they are all perfect at solving problems! It takes a lot of hard work to be able to form this degree of detachment!

The planets

One of the issues we often discuss with groups is the effect on problem-solving of what they feel strongly about. We do this by describing a model where each individual is a solar system. You are the sun at the centre and round you are a group of planets circulating, which constitute your satellite thoughts. The nearer your planets are to you the hotter they are, and the further away they are the cooler they are. The stronger you feel about something the larger the planet and vice versa. For example, you may feel very strongly about global warming and its effect on our Earth. You may have seen Al Gore's film *An Inconvenient Truth*, and have read widely on the issue. You therefore have a large red planet circling around your head. It is red because it is close to you and it is large because you have studied the subject. You may feel emotional but your emotions are well-informed ones. You are quite sure that the earth is warming up because of man-made CO_2 emissions and something has to be done to curb these, before it is too late.

Alternatively, you may feel strongly about global warming and know very little about it. In terms of problem-solving this would make a big difference because your feelings are not backed up with information. However, you just 'know' in your heart or intuitively that global warming is the biggest issue we have to deal with and we ought to do something about it. You are keen to put a halt to cheap air travel immediately and do not really care that an injustice might be caused which affected poorer people. This is a small red planet.

On the other hand, you may not feel strongly about global warming at all and know a lot about it. You may feel that the science has been hijacked, that the rise in the CO_2 output lags behind the Earth's temperature, that it all correlates with sunspot activity, that this is simply another of the changes that has frequently affected the Earth and that very little of it is man-made. This will affect the way you view the evidence and what should be done about it. You will have a large, blue planet circling your head. Finally, you might not care at all about climate change and your contribution to the argument will only be to complain vociferously when your freedoms are curtailed, and then you will move from having a very small blue planet to a very small red planet.

As you can see, what we reject or select has a big impact on how we approach the problem-solving arena. We are all prejudiced to some degree or another. In other words, we have all pre-judged the situation, which is what prejudice means. However, as we have demonstrated above concerning getting out of bed, approaching every situation in a completely new and fresh way would be very time-consuming. So the best that we can hope for is to realise that we approach any problem, no matter how trivial or large, with these deeply-seated ways of looking at the world built in, and that *so does everyone else*. We not only have our own biases to contend with, but everyone else's as well. We need to be aware that this is the case and try to delay, slow down and consider our judgement on issues. Only a bigot has no prejudices! 'Doubt is uncomfortable, but certainty is ridiculous', as Voltaire said.[3] We will be discussing this issue more when we come to consider values in Chapter 6. For a fuller description of 'mindset' we recommend Mark Brown's book, *The Dinosaur Strain*.[4]

What is cognitive style?

In the following part of this chapter we want to simplify some of the very complex ideas around cognitive style and convince you that here is something that you should know more about in relation to your team. We present a simple taxonomy or structure as to how you might see cognitive style and describe three ways of looking at it. The idea is to give you some practical things to work on for your own team. We also give some examples from our own experience. The important thing to bear in mind is that differences in cognitive style affect interpersonal functioning, and the way individuals interact with and relate to others.

First of all, a bit of history. Attempts to measure differences between the psychological characteristics of individuals can be traced back to 400 BC, when Hippocrates attempted to define four basic temperament types, each of which could be accounted for by a predominant body fluid or humour: blood – sanguine (optimistic); black bile – melancholic (depressed); yellow bile – choleric (irritable); and phlegm – phlegmatic (listless and sluggish).

Hippocrates' methods and the numerous other attempts at classification that have been made since then were hardly scientific, as we would now understand it.

The first attempt to measure the differences between individual mental abilities *scientifically* was made in the nineteenth century by Sir Francis Galton, who tried to show that the human mind could systematically be mapped into different dimensions. He studied, among other things, how people differed in terms of their ability to discriminate between stimuli, and by collating the results he obtained he devised a system which would allow an individual's abilities to be compared to those of others – an idea on which we rely heavily today in psychometric testing. From the work of people like Galton and his French contemporary, Binet, a picture of the human mental domain emerged which saw general human ability as being composed of a number of specific abilities[5] – a view which is still held today.

The concept of individual differences in the quality of cognitive functioning has been around since the birth of psychiatry in the early twentieth century. Cattell,[6] who was the British father of most early American psychometrics, used the concept, and even Jung had something to say on this issue. The term 'cognitive style' began its use with Allport in the 1930s.[7] There is no absolutely clear and agreed definition, but taking all the current ideas together, we can say it refers to an individual's characteristic and typically preferred mode of *processing* information. It is the manner in which individuals acquire, store and retrieve information or organise information. It influences how people look at their environment, and interpret it, and then how they use these interpretations for guiding their actions. Hence its great importance for team problem-solving. Many different theories about cognitive style exist not surprisingly as it is a basic principle of the way humans think and the basis of much of the psychometric testing industry. By 1994 more than a hundred instruments had already been developed for measuring individual differences and the dimensions on which cognitive style had been differentiated, and many more have been developed since then. You will be pleased to know that we are not going to discuss each one of these, but only the ones we think will be particularly helpful for team problem-solving.

Testing cognition

The concept behind psychometric testing in the work environment is that of enabling an employer to match the needs of the job to the skills and attitudes of a person, which is not always easy to do in an interview. Testing has mushroomed because, as Dr Kirton has said to us, 'If I am to work with you, I need to be able to predict how you are going to behave in a certain area. It would be impossible if you behaved differently every time we interacted.' Interviewing is time-consuming and open to bias. Giving someone a questionnaire saves time and prevents an accusation of prejudice being levelled at the interviewer.

It is vital to be able to understand and predict stable cognitive behaviour if a group of individuals is to work together as effective problem-solvers. It is important to understand that all prediction is based on preference – preference equals practice equals performance. This point about preference is an important one and is rarely explained to people undertaking psychometric tests. All a test can do is reflect back to you what you say you prefer. By understanding an individual's preferences we are able to predict their likely behaviour in certain circumstances more accurately than via any other method. If people like doing something they usually do it regularly and then they become good at it. The opposite isn't necessarily true, and we have come across people at conferences who were trapped in work they disliked because they had been found to be good at it and they dared not admit their true feelings in case they lost their job.

We have already seen in Chapter 2 that an individual in a group of social mammals has two opposing urges: to be accepted by its peers, and to fulfil a set of more basic drives such as those for water, food, cover, warmth, sex, territory, etc. This opposition has been described as the 'anxiety provoked by perceived annihilation in membership on the one hand and separation and loss of affiliation on the other'.[8] It is not surprising, then, that one of the first polarities that emerges in any results is that of analytic/holistic.

In order to understand how cognitive style is able to help with team problem-solving, we are going to approach it at different levels of complexity, depending on what it is you want to do with it. Our hierarchy of complexity works something like this. The first level of cognitive style is instructional preference – that is, how you like to receive information. This is easily influenced by the surrounding environment and is not very stable, but it is relevant for our purposes, because you may approach problem-solving in your team wanting individuals to be able to minimise their weaknesses. Information processing is somewhat more stable but can be affected by learning strategies. We are going to look at this in terms of right and left brain difference. The pure cognitive style which is the most stable is the consistent mode which individuals show in their perceptual and intellectual activities. We are going to look at this in terms of Dr Kirton's adaption and innovation theory.

Learning theory

We have already seen in Chapter 2 that Gagné[9] coupled together problem-solving and learning. It is therefore not surprising that one of the most original pieces of work on cognition was that done on learning styles by David Kolb.[10] Kolb's theory suggests that the way the mind works is by following a circle or spiral through

registering a situation (concrete experience)
thinking about it (reflective observation)
forming a theory (abstract conceptualisation)
and then *acting* (active experimentation)

when the cycle begins again.

Under Kolb's theory you fell into a quadrant on two of these axes. You were a 'Diverger' (someone who opened the problem up), an 'Assimilator' (someone who was keen to understand why things happened the way they did and formulate a generalised theory that would apply), a 'Converger' (someone who focused any ideas down to a manageable number and then made a choice), or an 'Accommodator' (someone who got on and did what was required). When we were using this theory we tended to describe it in terms of the colours that we used for our problem-tackling model (see Chapter 4). Thus Divergers were blue, for blue sky ideas, Assimilators were red, for careful scrutiny, Convergers were blue and red because they had both conceptual thinking and analysis, and Accommodators were green for get up and go. (For access to Kolb's Learning Style questionnaire, go to www.learningfromexperience.com.)

Kolb's ideas were developed by Honey and Mumford,[11] who felt that to ascribe individuals to one of these quadrants was too limiting. They wanted a more accurate measure of where you were on each of the different scales. Thus their four scales refer to Reflectors, Theorists, Pragmatists and Activists, and by completing their Learning Styles questionnaire you can see where you are on the four scales. Completing the questionnaire is quick and easy. A full online version of this questionnaire is available from www.peterhoney.com on a pay-as-you-go basis. The results come as a full report with suggestions about how to become a more effective learner. Although geared to the individual, the reports can easily be adapted to a team context, especially where problems have been experienced between team members.

Why is learning theory important for teams?

Why is learning styles theory important for teams? We have already seen how close problem-solving and learning styles are. If all the members of a team are strong Reflectors, the chances are that they will not cover the remainder of the cycle and get round to doing anything. They will be too happy opening things up and thinking about things. You can imagine that a group of research and development people might behave like this. They will continue to puzzle over things for as long as they can, but they will not necessarily come up with a solution that is practicable unless they are forced into doing so. If, on the other hand you had a group of Activists then the converse would be true. They are likely to dash into activity without really thinking the problem through or searching all avenues or coming up with a plan that they all agree on. It would be too simple to say that a team should have strengths in all the categories. It rather depends on what the team is there to do. However, an understanding of learning theory and what each of the learning styles is like can be a great help to a team that is struggling, because it develops a language and presents an opportunity for dialogue and discussion. Sometimes 'personality problems' can be explained in this way.

People who are in opposite quadrants or strong on opposite lines tend to see the world in a different way from each other, so that not surprisingly they need help when trying to work out where the other, diametrically opposed, person is coming from.

Once individuals understand their own style and that of other team members, they begin to see how the learning styles can best be used. Most problems need to be explored at the outset and looked at from different perspectives. Reflectors comes into their own at this stage. 'Why is this like this?' requires more analytical skills, and this is where Theorists comes into their own. They think problems through in a step-by-step way. Pragmatists are keen to focus down on to a solution, so they will want something that is practical that they can work on. Activists like to get stuck in, especially if the experience is new to them. They like working with others, especially if they can do so from the front. If a problem can be broken down into these phases and the appropriate person is enabled to use their skills in the most useful way then it is likely that the problem will be tackled much more effectively.

One of the important things about learning styles is that individuals can get better at them. You can take two different approaches to this. You can look at your team and the strengths and weaknesses that it has in terms of learning styles. If you have a spread of styles that match the type of problems you have then you can simply do what we have suggested above and make sure that the person with the appropriate skill leads at the appropriate time. Using this route individuals keep on developing their strengths. However, you could also take the view that someone from the team might leave and carry out an analysis to make sure that you would still be covered if that were the case. That might mean people attempting to improve on their less strong traits. The Honey and Mumford book is helpful in suggesting ways in which people might improve on their learning styles.[12] If you cannot cover the necessary styles in your existing team then you are going to have to work with your team to make sure that you can cover all the styles if necessary, or recruit a new person with the requisite skills.

Sometimes it is possible to look at large groups of people and make an assessment as to whether the group as a whole has a weakness. While running a conference of around a hundred people for a large children's charity, one of the things we asked them to do was to complete the Kolb Learning Styles questionnaire. The results made it clear that as an organisation they had Divergers, Convergers and Accommodators but no Assimilators. In other words, they had plenty of people with good ideas, many people who wanted to focus on a solution and lots of people who wanted to get into action. What they did not have were people who wanted to know why things happened the way they did and come up with a generalised theory as to why this was so. Now you may say this is not surprising. A children's charity needs to get on and do things. However, on reflection you might appreciate that they also had no one who was checking what they were doing and stopping them making the same mistakes twice. How did they know whether or not a certain action was successful or effective? How did they know that they were spending money wisely? Having completed the Learning Styles questionnaire and having found this weakness out, they could think about whether they wanted to do anything about it.

We encountered another example of a gap in the cycle while we were working for a packaging design company in Brussels. This company had plenty of every colour except the red of the Assimilator. There was no one who was there to make rules and see that they were kept. As a result the organisation was rather anarchic and costs were out of control. They realised that they needed people like this, but wondered how long they would last if they managed to recruit them.

Right brain and left brain theories

Researchers in the 1960s made some astonishing discoveries about the brain and how it worked. In a drastic treatment for epilepsy, surgeons had operated on a number of patients by cutting the *corpus callosum* – the thick bundle of nerve fibres that forms the main connection between the two cerebral hemispheres of the brain. What this action seemed to reveal was two types of brain activity – the left-hand side had speech and a rational, intellectual approach, while the right-hand side was speechless, but was blessed with special spatial abilities and appeared to be more creative. Thus, in a test for patients who had undergone this type of surgery, the left brain would connect to a picture of a fork and a spoon when the patient saw a cake on a plate, while the right brain would select a picture of a broad-brimmed hat. The left brain was matching for function while the right brain would match by appearance or association, and apparently had a lot more fun in the process!

With advances in technology and brain-scanning equipment, a different picture has emerged. This shows that both sides of the brain play an active part in these processes. Language turns out to be represented on both sides of the brain. The left deals with such aspects as grammar and word production, while the right is involved in emphasis and intonation. The right side focuses on the broad background picture and is good at seeing general connections, while the left deals with objects in a particular location.[13] The conclusion seems to be that the two hemispheres differ in their processing styles rather than in terms of what they are processing. Perhaps even more amazingly, these tests have been reproduced with chimps. In other words, a division of labour between the two sides of the brain seems to have been a good thing long before human beings came along. Now it is believed that every mental faculty is shared across the brain, with each side contributing in a complementary, not exclusive, fashion. Another fascinating finding from people who have had strokes on the right side of the brain is that when presented with a saying such as 'A stitch in time saves nine', they can only relate it to sewing and cannot 'see' its wider implications. The right side does indeed seem to have a more playful capacity.

This may be fascinating, but what are the implications for people working in teams? There is still evidence that while the brain is not quite as simplified in its functions as we may have thought, different people do still favour different sides. A member of your team whose strengths are on the left, for example, may not see or appreciate the playful allusions of someone whose strength is on the right, who in turn may not have the precision of the person on the left. As we shall see in the next chapter on creativity, being able to make associations across a wide area can be very useful in certain brainstorming-type exercises, while in other circumstances precision is what is required.

Again, it is about appropriateness, and it is in respecting

difference that the most effective team problem-solving lies. You can have some fun with your team by downloading some questionnaires from the Web (try www.singsurf.org/brian/rightbrain.php) and discussing the results. Always take these tests with a pinch of salt bearing in mind that research is changing our knowledge of how the brain functions all the time, as can be seen from the above discussion. Today's certainties are tomorrow's heresies. The important thing is to discuss issues of this nature with your team and discover if anything fruitful comes from it.

Just as a postscript, another aspect to this left and right business is that of left hand and right hand orientation. A useful prize-winning book on this issue is Chris McManus's *Right Hand, Left Hand*.

Adaption-Innovation theory

The concept we feel is most useful for an understanding of what goes wrong in teams when it comes to problem solution is the Adaption-Innovation theory which has been created and developed by Dr Michael Kirton.[14] An important component of this theory is that it does not conflate (mix up) style with ability. The related measurement tool, known as the Kirton Adaption Innovation Inventory, does not measure individual *ability* in problem-solving, and will not reflect how good a person is at solving problems. What it does demonstrate is the way they usually go about doing so – in other words, their problem-solving style. In the next chapter, we will be writing about how this affects creativity and attitudes to it, but here we are just talking about the way in which people solve problems.

Dr Kirton distinguishes two styles which together form a continuum. The two approaches are called the adaptive and the innovative. The styles are relative. One person is always more adaptive or more innovative than another in any situation.

In the main, the more adaptive problem-solver works within the paradigm constraints in which the problem was set, and prefers to do things 'better', using structure as a resource. This type will generally be patient, prudent and careful, will implement change only when supported by others, and will move more incrementally towards the desired goal. Problems will be solved within the nature of the paradigm in which the question was posed. These people generally get on well with their fellow team members. They do not produce huge numbers of ideas, but if they are intelligent enough will produce a few really good ones that will solve the problem. If they are true to type, they are generally quite efficient and only challenge the rules with good reason. They do not set out with the attention of breaking them. The more adaptive are geared towards challenges and threats from inside the organisation.

Most large organisations are adaptive. In times of stability they work extremely well and the shareholders are kept happy by the steady progression of the share price. Would you describe your organisation like this?

The more innovative problem-solver works across and between paradigms and prefers to do things 'differently', despite the surrounding structure, which might be seen as hampering. This type will take more risks, be disruptive and be unaware of any need for group cohesion. While the more adaptive will accuse the more innovative of breaking the rules, the latter will simply say that they are challenging or reinterpreting them and that the rules are only there as a guide. The more innovative are geared towards challenges and threats from outside the organisation. In times of instability and turbulence being adaptive is rarely enough, and it is at this stage that organisations tend to look around for the innovative types to provide solutions to their problems.

When the two types collaborate they bring a wide spectrum of approaches to all the problems teams have to solve. This collaboration also involves appreciating whose approach is the most appropriate for the specific problem posed. That is why it is important to have a mix of styles in any group. When team members do not collaborate, much time and energy is spent, particularly by the leader, in trying to manage them.

One of our very first examples of the problems that people from the different ends of the spectrum could provide for the leader of the group was from a board of directors in Scandinavia. This particular organisation was in insurance and pensions. They were very successful in promoting their products and had a 26 per cent market share. Their dilemma was how to grow the business, as gaining further market share was difficult with existing products and services. The marketing director had identified what he thought was a very lucrative market for the company's products in one recently emerging member of the EEC. He could see that an opportunity existed to export know-how to countries where the market was underdeveloped. He suggested to the board that they immediately began a big marketing push to sell their insurance and pension products in his target country. He saw this as a great opportunity that should not be missed. You may have realised that he was from the more innovative end of the spectrum. Meanwhile the actuary, who had contributed greatly to the success of the organisation by accurately predicting actuarial rates and therefore making profits, was tearing his hair out. In vain did he point out that he did not have sufficient data for this new market and therefore was unable to predict how it was likely to behave. He felt that going down this route was too much of a risk for the company to take. He simply was unable to communicate sufficiently his great sense of unease. You may appreciate that this man was from the more adaptive end of the spectrum. The two were a very long way apart in terms of their problem-solving style. The marketing man was acting true to his type and so was the actuary. In fact, you probably would not want to employ a marketing person who was over-cautious or an actuary who thought that it is a good idea to bet your insurance money on the dogs. The managing director, who was a 'bridger' in the middle (see below), was left with the problem of sorting out what the organisation's future policy should be. As far as we know they did not expand into this new market but grew organically by forming alliances with other companies.

From this story you might be led into the erroneous impression that all professions such as marketers and actuaries will always be the same in terms of their adaptive or innovative approaches to problem-solving. Not so. In fact, there will always be a distribution, but the mean of that distribution will usually cluster around being either more adaptive or more innovative. However, it is true to say that there will always be groupings of different types of style around specific departments within organisations. No organisation produces a total uniformity of cognitive style. The more adaptive styles tend to be found in parts of a company that need to concentrate on problems arising from within their own department, such as production, while the more innovative styles tend to be found in those areas of the organisation that face problems from outside their department, such as sales. This may explain some of the conflicts that traditionally arise between different parts of an organisation, such as production and marketing, for example.

Bridgers

It is important that we refer to people as 'more adaptive' and 'more innovative' because the concept will always be relative. In any group the normal distribution will cover people from both ends of the spectrum, with some people in the middle, but the group itself could be at either the innovative or the adaptive end of the spectrum. The people in the middle of the group, *wherever it is placed*, are 'bridgers' and they fulfil a very important function. They are important because they are more likely to be able to understand the point of view of people from both ends of the spectrum and attempt to reconcile their differences. However, if the distance is too great there will be just as large a gulf between some team members and the bridger as between the two ends of the team's spectrum. We have worked with teams which have included a very innovative leader and members who were highly adaptive. In their exasperation with and non-comprehension of the important role played by the more adaptive members of their team, the leader has abrogated responsibility for these people and has asked a senior member of the team to act as a bridger/go-between.

If a more adaptive individual chairs a meeting, it is likely that all the items on the agenda will be covered and that the more innovative members will feel that not enough time is given to exploring some ideas thoroughly. They will come away from the meeting disgruntled. If a more innovative person chairs a meeting, the agenda is unlikely to be covered and the adaptors will be very upset that they are coming away from the meeting with items that have not been covered at all. If a bridger chairs a meeting, either both ends of the spectrum will be dissatisfied or they will be reasonably happy. Where do you lie on this spectrum? Do you chair team meetings? It is sometimes useful to allocate time to certain topics that need debate and then move on.

One of our consultancy projects entailed setting up problem-solving teams to cover all newspaper titles published by a provincial newspaper group over a wide geographical area. This amounted to twenty-one teams. We kicked this project off by holding a seminar for all interested staff at each newspaper, explaining the theory and what we wanted to achieve. We then asked staff members to participate. From those who did we were able to set up teams balanced between the more adaptive and the more innovative. People who had not got on with one another suddenly realised how they could help each other. If there is a desire to communicate and a pay-off, people will do so. People with very different problem-solving styles formed strong bonds and useful, lasting working partnerships because they valued what the other person had to offer. These teams produced many good ideas for promoting the papers from both inside and outside the paradigm, which affected the bottom line positively.

Never underestimate the more adaptive!

It is a common myth, believed by many people in organisations and not a few of our own colleagues, that what we are looking for in order to make far-reaching changes, is *only* the more innovative problem-solving style of person. This has led to people in organisations who have a more adaptive style feeling that being innovative is what they should strive for, as it appears so much more glamorous and has the added benefit of being rewarded by management. Although it is not true to say that more innovative people have no staying power (if sufficiently motivated, they can focus very hard and pay attention to detail), this is largely coping behaviour and is costly in terms of energy. Relying only on the more innovative style to carry change through is a miscalculation on the part of management, which can also alienate the adaptive section of the workforce and may make them switch off completely. It can also lead people into thinking that they can manipulate the outcomes when completing the questionnaire. However, this distortion is nearly always observable by the person analysing it.

People with highly innovative styles often tend to lose interest in new ideas when it comes to making them happen. They enjoyed generating the ideas but they then want to get on to the next novel and interesting problem. If the innovative idea is the one that is going to solve a particular problem, then the more innovative have to persuade the more adaptive that it is worth spending time on. The more adaptive will then get on and make it work, by putting in the systems and structures. This is one of the reasons some innovative types who are fantastic salespersons may be less than good at completing the paperwork. If this is the case, it is a bit pointless making them do it when they could be out there achieving more sales. There are some people who simply love the paperwork and enjoy the detail for its intrinsic interest. Nothing pleases them more than having neat and tidy records. If you can get these two types to co-operate and help each other to achieve results then you are on your way to having a productive and happy workforce. However, if you embark on this type of division of labour, it is vitally important to reward those who keep the records as well as those who make the sales, as the former are taking off a burden from those in sales. What often happens is that the salesperson is rewarded, leaving the form-filler rightly feeling aggrieved.

Precipitating events

Change is often brought about when an event occurs that brings home, forcibly and dramatically, the need for change to a person or a group of people. This event can be described as a precipitating event. It is a trait of the more adaptive and more innovative that they are able to see this precipitating event in different timescales.[15]

The more innovative are able to see the event a long way off and to warn of its consequences. Unfortunately, because it cannot be seen by the more adaptive members of the team (rather like a tsunami), these warnings are inclined to be ignored. More adaptive types recognise precipitating events much later, and sometimes when nothing can be done about what is about to happen.

At one stage, we were working for a group in America who had been given a project involved with recruitment. It was clear to us that, unless they proved themselves useful and cost-effective in a short space of time, their budget would be withdrawn. However, we could not prevail upon the group to appreciate the peril they were in. We were present when the bad news was broken to them. It came as a complete shock – they had been too busy to notice the looming catastrophe.

A conference we ran for an insurance company showed that the profile of attendees was skewed to a more innovative style and they were aware that they needed to change, because speaker after speaker told them so. However, the attendees' profile (and their perception of the need for change) was not shared by the senior management who had by contrast a more adaptive style, and within five years the company was no more. Often, organisations need to change when they are at their most successful, but are held back because those with the most to lose think, if there is nothing wrong, why fix it? This is where the person with a more innovative style will see the precipitating event on the horizon but cannot persuade those with a more adaptive style that it is there. This is often called 'the failure of success'.

It is very useful to have a person in your team who can recognise a precipitating event very early on. However, it is often very difficult to admit that such is the case if you do not yourself have a more innovative style. You may think that they are imagining things, or that they are exaggerating or making things up just to get your attention. All such warnings should be examined with some degree of depth. If they are found to have been worthless this may make the precipitating person more careful as to what they bring to your attention in future. However, you must not scare them off. One day they will be absolutely right and you will have to take notice of them.

Organisation life histories

Organisations tend to start off being innovative. They are full of ideas, rule-challenging and flexible. As time goes by they need people to make rules and process the paperwork and generally stop the wheels falling off. These people gradually gain more power and the organisation becomes less responsive and gradually over time people forget what the organisation's *raison d'être* was in the first place. In the worst cases an organisation is so busy keeping itself alive and its people are so keen to protect their jobs that it simply implodes. Vicere has shown this very comprehensively in an article which demonstrates that unless organisations rediscover their reason for existence they simply become more and more bureaucratic.[16] The organisations he suggests (BP, GE, Conrail) might or might not be the ones that come to mind now (he wrote his paper in 1991), which reinforces the concept that organisations wax and wane in terms of their ability to cope with their environment.

Making the theory work for you

We hope that, having read the above, you will understand more about Dr Kirton's theory, and that it makes sense to you. It is important to have an understanding of your own perspective, whether adaptive or innovative, and of how this affects your relationship with others in your team. If you feel isolated you may have to make special efforts to communicate with others in your team. If you are the leader this may cast light on some of your difficulties. You may have to find someone to act as a bridger to individuals who are very different from you. You can become skilled in administering the KAI inventory (ukinfo@kaicentre.com) or find someone accredited like us who would be happy to work with you and your team.

Summary

What we have tried to do in this chapter is convince you of the importance of different problem-solving styles for the effectiveness of your team. We have shown that different perceptions, although often difficult to accommodate, have great merits in enabling us to solve different sorts of problems. Most particularly we want to demonstrate that a combination of styles is the most effective. We have introduced you to cognitive style and discussed different examples of it, including learning styles, left and right brain theories and the Adaption and Innovation theory. In the latter, we have given examples of precipitating events.

In the next chapter, we go on to look at the power of creativity and we have a few contentious things to say about it! We believe that everyone is creative, but with different styles and with different outcomes. What does this mean in terms of how teams solve problems?

What can you do about the power of problem-solving style?

- Think about the other members of your team. Is there someone whose style is very different from yours? Do you find this difficult to accommodate? Can you think of an example when their approach was better at solving a problem than yours? How could you divide up problems between you so that you could both use your appropriate styles?

- Can you give an example of 'selective seeing' from your own experience – for example, buying a car, or when a new word popped up several times over a short space of time?

- Can you name some of your own 'planets'? Are they big or small, hot or cold? How do you think these affect other team members?

- Would it be useful to discuss learning theory with your team? Why not try the Honey and Mumford questionnaire?

- Why not discuss left brain theories with your team? Do you have people in your team who seem to favour one or the other? What effect does this have on the way you work together?

- When you chair a meeting what sort of style do you adopt? Do you leave anyone frustrated? How can you change this?

- Do you have someone on your team who is trying to warn you of precipitating events and are you listening? Conversely, are you trying to fulfil this function with your team?

- Do you think it would be useful to become accredited to administer the Kirton Adaption and Innovation (KAI) inventory or to find someone accredited to use with your team?

Notes

[1] http://www.dgsgardening.btinternet.co.uk/convertlength.htm, last accessed 10 Aug. 2007.

[2] Brown, M. (1988) *The Dinosaur Strain* (Shaftsbury, Dorset: Element Books).

[3] We think this is Voltaire, but if you know something different please let us know.

[4] Brown, M. (1988) *The Dinosaur Strain* (Shaftsbury, Dorset: Element Books).

[5] Bulmer, Michael, (2003), *Francis Galton: Pioneer of Heredity and Biometry*, John Hopkins University Press

[6] Cattell, R. B. (1957) *Personality and Motivation: Structure and Measurement* (Yonkers-on-Hudson: World Book Co.).

[7] Allport, G. W. and Vernon, P. E. (1931) *A Study of Values* (Boston, MA: Houghton Mifflin).

[8] Kreps, J. I. (2006) 'Anxiety', *Islamica*, 18.

[9] Gagné, R. M. (1974) 'Problem Solving and Thinking', *Annual Review of Psychology*, 10.

[10] Kolb, D. A. (1984) *Experiential Learning: Experience as the Source of Learning and Development* (Englewood Cliffs, NJ: Prentice-Hall).

[11] Honey, P. and Mumford, A. (1982) *The Manual of Learning Styles* (Maidenhead: Peter Honey Publications).

[12] www.honeyandmumford.co.uk

[13] See McCrone, J. (2000) '"Right brain" or "left brain": myth or reality?', http://www.rense.com/general2/rb.htm [originally pub. *New Scientist*, 3 Jul. 1999].

[14] Kirton, M. J. (ed.) (1994) *Adaptors and Innovators: Styles of Creativity and Problem-solving* (London: Routledge), rev. pbk edn.

[15] ibid.

[16] Vicere, A. A. (1991) 'The strategic leadership imperative for executive development', *Human Resource Planning*, vol. 15, issue 1, pp. 15–31.

4

The Power of Creativity

Introduction

This chapter is about the power of creativity and how the different creative styles of the individuals in a team can both help and hinder the effectiveness of the team's problem-solving. After discussing the origins of creativity and modern approaches both to it and to its corollary, improvements and innovations, we will argue that everyone is creative, with their own creative style, and that all these styles of creativity can make a contribution to a team. Many people associate creativity with artistic ability, such as painting, sculpture, pottery, writing, etc. These are outcomes relating to capability of a very particular nature, whereas style is about the way you go about doing something.

What does creativity mean

An ancient Hebrew definition of 'creativity' would seem to imply that creativity concerns the making of life out of nothing and is therefore the sole prerogative of God. There matters seem to have been left until our more scientific age, when Koestler[1] poured cold water on the aim of prediction or measurability by declaring that creativity was not something possessed by ordinary people or understood by them. Opinions vary as to whether you need a high Intelligence Quotient (IQ). The figure of 120-plus is sometimes mentioned, which seems to indicate that, as the average for the population is 100, the majority of people can never hope to be creative. Other studies have shown that there is no correlation at all between high IQ and creativity except that a certain level of IQ is needed, but how high/low is this? One of the biggest problems concerns who judges the output, which is presumably how the level of creativity is arrived at. Would different people, themselves at different creative levels, come to different conclusions? We only have to look at modern 'conceptual' art to know this to be true from our own experience and reactions. While some people would not see a pickled shark as creative in terms of output, Damien Hirst is laughing all the way to the bank. People may look at the artwork and think, 'I could do that', but admirers of the work would argue they are missing the point, that it is the concept that is valued, not the ability to put it into practice.

There have always been creative managers. The industrial revolution was fathered by scientists and engineers who pioneered the new technologies. They sought solutions to the social, political, economic, scientific and technological problems of an industrialising society. The Founding Fathers of the United States of America had a vision which encompassed freeing themselves from the outdated political thinking of Europe with a government that served the people rather than the other way round. Creative managers founded the Royal Society of London for Improving Knowledge where men of like ability came together to discuss their ideas.[2] What these men had in common was this huge desire to improve things and make a difference. Does your team have this hunger for change? What new challenges does it face?

But, if we know the results of creativity when we see them, what does being creative mean and how do we go about it? The management literature is simply awash with hundreds of different definitions of what constitutes 'creativity', most of them conflating (i.e. mixing up) style and ability, and there is no consensus. There have been attempts to find an agreed definition. One idea was that creative thinking should lead to tangible products, or something that is new, or exclude something that is not valuable. Dr Kirton has summed the situation up in writing:

> Many of the distinctions come through differences in what is the main focus of the definition, whether it is the entity undertaking the creativity, the process that is used in its operation, the outcome of the process, or the evaluation from the environment in which it all exists[3].

What is astonishing is that as far back as 1950 psychologists were saying that creative acts can be expected, even if feeble and infrequently, from almost all individuals. Sadly, that suggestion has been ignored in favour of elitism. Now many people in organisations and outside want to label only a favoured few as 'creative'.

Another complication is caused by the word 'innovation', which has come into vogue with an equally vague definition that overlaps with creativity to the point where the two terms are often synonymous.

Our idea of creativity

The answer lies in accepting that creativity is a function of style and that we all have different styles. This then leads naturally to the idea that we are all creative. Creativity is a subset of problem-solving, of which innovation is at one end of a continuum of style. Everyone can problem-solve and be creative: they just do so with different styles and different outcomes. Every style may be appropriate to some problems but not to others – so all styles can make a contribution, more so on some occasions than others, depending on the type of problem being addressed. No one is comfortable for long with problems that require a different style for their resolution from the one they prefer. There is such a thing as coping behaviour, but it uses up valuable energy and cannot be sustained for long periods. (We will be returning to this issue later in this chapter when we discuss how to integrate styles and get individuals in the team to work together.)

There are many benefits to be had from this line of thinking. The first is that it overcomes an inferiority complex, which often afflicts individuals in all walks of life who will tell you that they are not creative. This usually means that they do not see themselves in an artistic capacity. However, they are all capable of managing their lives and finding solutions to their own domestic problems in a satisfying way. They are all capable of change and functioning adequately in a world that is constantly changing around them, and as we shall see below have an important function in making change happen.

Secondly, there are some people who have been led to believe that there are other members of the organisation who are the 'creative' ones, and whose jobs are much more glamorous than those of the 'work-horses' in the back office. These so-called 'creative' people receive much more praise, recognition and reward, and are held up for emulation. This is particularly so when a major change programme is in the air. These people are sought out and held up as the type of person the organisation needs at this point in its evolution. This often leads to great distress on the part of those many individuals who are led to believe that their contribution is no longer worthwhile. As there are many of them in most organisations (as organisations are generally adaptive in nature), morale tends to plummet. If your team is planning a major change, your strategy should include keeping the more adaptive types happy and smiling at all times. They will not be the early adopters of change, and much effort should go into persuading them that change is necessary. However, once persuaded they will put their muscle behind your ideas and will make sure that change happens, while the early adopters may have drifted on to other things that appear more novel.

We once ran a conference for the top pyramid of a television company – about sixty people. Most delegates present had a title with 'Creative' in it, except the maintenance people. With our views on creativity the more adaptive members of the organisation had the chance to fight back. Giving people a title with 'Creative' in it merely signals that you think everyone else is not creative. This is not a good way to get the best from team members and you may be surprised how much resentment smoulders in these circumstances.

Thirdly, it is of crucial importance that people with different styles of creativity appreciate the help they can give one another. By working together they can solve a range of problems not open to just one type or style of creativity. Thus everyone is valued for what they can contribute.

What are the different styles of creativity

The styles of creativity range along a continuum from more adaptive to more innovative.[4] This theory has been described in more detail in Chapter 3.

In summary, an individual with a more adaptive creative style works within the paradigm and prefers to do things 'better', using structure as a resource. This type will be patient, prudent and careful, implement change only when supported by others, and generally move more incrementally towards the desired goal. Problems will be solved within the nature of the paradigm in which the question was posed. These people generally get on well with their fellow team members. They do not produce huge numbers of ideas but if they are intelligent enough will produce a few really good ones that will solve the problem. If they are true to type, they are generally quite efficient and only challenge the rules with good reason. They do not set out with the attention of breaking them. The Japanese are brilliant exponents of this type of creativity. They continually improve their products and services incrementally, that is in small steps. How many different types of Sony Walkman are there? (And did you know that it was originally designed to stop its inventor annoying other people with his music choice?)

The individual with the more innovative creative style works across and between paradigms and prefers to do things 'differently', despite the surrounding structure, which might be seen as hampering. This type will take more risks, be disruptive and be unaware of any need for group cohesion. While the more adaptive will accuse the more innovative of breaking the rules, the latter will simply say that they are challenging or reinterpreting them and that the rules are only there as a guide. The more adaptive are geared towards challenges and threats from inside while the more innovative are geared towards challenges and threats from outside. The British are good at this type of creativity – making a change outside the original paradigm. The steam engine, the jet, the railway, the hovercraft are all products which required a leap of the imagination. However, we are not so good at seeing the commercial potential of these ideas and other people often develop them in a way we had not foreseen, thereby making money out of them.

Of course, the question is often asked – who is the most creative, an adaptor or an innovator? Dr Kirton cites the example of Howard Carter, who is well-known for his discovery of the tomb of Tutankhamen. The way Carter found the tomb where others had failed is often described as having involved some sort of intuitive guesswork.

Far from it. Carter used a grid system to cover the area of the desert where he thought it likely the tomb might be, and specifically looked for areas of depression where there might have been substantial diggings. He tried many areas of his grid before he found what he was looking for. Once inside the tomb Carter worked painstakingly to ensure that the objects were taken out from above with as little disturbance as possible and that careful records were kept of where all the artefacts had been placed. He didn't just jump into the tomb area and start handing things up willy-nilly to his amazed assistants. So was Carter an innovator or an adaptor? Dr Kirton believes he was an intelligent well-trained adaptor and that this example demonstrates that intelligent adaptors can be just as creative, if not more so, than innovators. Innovators, once they have had their ideas, tend to lose interest and want to move on to the next thing before they have put into effect the results of their thinking. This does not always happen as there are people with a more innovative creative style who can pay attention to detail and be very professional in completing the task. However, in many instances they lack the long-term persistence and patience necessary to carry a change through to its end. As a result, they nearly always have to convince more adaptive people of the possibilities of their ideas before things really get moving. Once a more adaptive person is on board, the more innovative can be sure that their ideas will come to fruition.

How can you use the creativity in your team

You have probably attended a course, or been involved in a team, where someone has suggested that you 'brainstorm' ideas in order to solve a problem that you may have. With no more ado, someone grabs the pen and you all stand around the flipchart board and shout out solutions. Depending on your own creative style you will either have enjoyed this enormously or have felt acute embarrassment and remained silent. If you have had to do this frequently you may have got better at it, but the unstructured way in which it is done and the rather dubious results may not have encouraged you to try it with your own team, or if you have the results might not have been encouraging. Quantity does not necessarily mean quality.

This type of exercise makes certain assumptions. The first is that an unstructured session like this is 'creative' and that everyone can do it or learn to do it. Many fortunes have been built on the idea of 'making you more creative'. In fact we discussed some of this in the last chapter on the left- and right-side aspects of the brain, much of which is now discredited and itself has boiled down to a matter of style and process.

The truth is that you *can* learn to be creative in a way that does not necessarily represent your natural style. We have for a long time had a client who, while not having an innovative style, is able to run an innovative technique of brainstorming almost as well as we can, because he has seen us do it so many times that he has learnt the drill.

However, as we have explained earlier, this is an example of 'coping behaviour' and is costly in terms of energy. Why learn another style when you have a perfectly good style of your own that can be harnessed to produce ideas? Why not let those who like producing ideas for the sake of it, and making connections across paradigms, have the chance to do it and enjoy themselves, while those with a more adaptive style use techniques which favour their style so they too can enjoy themselves? In other words, it is 'horses for courses'. There is no reason to make people feel uncomfortable and switch them off. They can make a contribution within their own comfort zone.

What follows is a simple model for tackling problems which utilises all of the strengths of the individuals in your team and enables each person to play their part. It uses colour to bring the process alive. Colour has been associated with the right brain (see Chapter 3) and helps the brain to associate ideas and function more effectively. Most people would prefer to have a colour television than a black and white one (although it's true that, on occasion, black and white can be more dramatic). In many ways it does not matter what colours you use. You may prefer the colours from Edward de Bono's *Six Thinking Hats*,[5] for example. We use blue, red and green, in the way described below.

The Colour Spectrum

There is nothing wrong with brainstorming, but it needs to occur in a structured context. Teams sitting down to resolve problems and explore opportunities can be extremely chaotic – everyone has their own view of how to approach the situation and a lot of time and energy are wasted as a result (see Chapters 2 and 3). What follows is a model – the Colour Spectrum – which enables a team to use a common language and comprises a structured approach to team problem-tackling. This model also takes into account that there is always a ghostly presence in the room where the team is working – those people whom you have to influence if the team is to move ahead. You have to think carefully about who these people are.

The Spectrum is designed to utilise all the different styles of creativity in the team and is intended to be worked through from left to right. However, you may find that the component parts are equally useful on occasions and can be used on their own. Below you will see a diagram of the model (Figure 9). The colours are important. They represent *blue* sky thinking, *red* for let's stop and think about this, and *green* for goal selection and action. We will now proceed to explain the Colour Spectrum in more detail so that you can use the model yourself with your team.

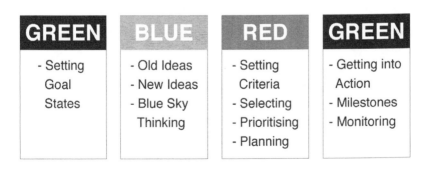

GREEN
- Setting Goal States

BLUE
- Old Ideas
- New Ideas
- Blue Sky Thinking

RED
- Setting Criteria
- Selecting
- Prioritising
- Planning

GREEN
- Getting into Action
- Milestones
- Monitoring

Figure 9. The Colour Spectrum

One of the most important points to bear in mind is that the different creative styles of the individuals in the team will match different parts of the model. The trick is to use the person with the appropriate style at the appropriate part of the model. That is why diversity in a team is so important. You can use some of the information that we have already discussed in Chapter 3, relating to the different learning styles or problem-solving styles, to determine the strengths of your team members. In summary, the person in your team who generates the most ideas will be useful in the (blue) section on ideas, but so will the people who generate a few sound ideas. We will explain this in more detail shortly. The person who always considers things very carefully, has lots of 'yes, but ...'s to say, will be very useful in the (red) criteria and selection phases, and the person who can't wait to get on with things will be very useful in the (green) goal selection and action phases.

Before you start looking at how to work through the Colour Spectrum you might like to spend a few minutes thinking about your team in the above terms (i.e. from what you know already), matching individual styles to the model. For example, you might have a lot of 'red' thinkers, people who close down on a solution very early and do not think widely enough. You may think that you have a lot of people with ideas – so much so that they never get down to any action. This will indicate where you might expect your team to spend a disproportionate amount of time and will remind you to correct it. People will always rest in their comfort zone, given the opportunity, and it is the role of the leader to ensure that this does not happen (i.e. that your team do not have favourite parts of the model that they linger over).

Stage 1: Analysing the problem

Before starting to work the model (Figure 9) it is important to make sure that there has been sufficient analysis of the problem. All views are important at this stage because this is where you discover that everyone has a different idea of what the problem you are trying to solve is really about – that is, there is a lot of unshared uncertainty. (See the sections in Chapter 2 on perception and mindset.) The first thing to do is to get all the available information out of everyone's head and into a tangible form. There are several methods you can use. If you and your team are familiar with mind-mapping it may be helpful to draw a giant mind-map that can be added to over days and even weeks.[6] Mind-maps are essentially dynamic, fluid and visual, and can also be colourful in order to activate the right side of the brain. They can often be better than lists or descriptions in making connections between disparate ideas. Start with Opportunities, Issues and Problems as your main branches and build out from there (Figure 10).

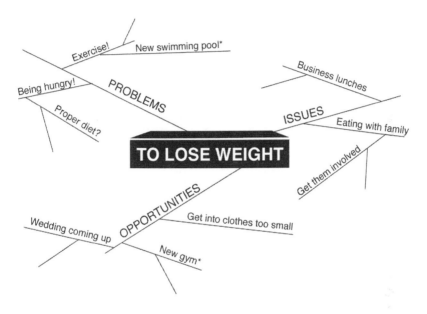

Figure 10. Mind Map

Alternatively, you could ask each person to describe the problem as they see it and get all the thoughts down on a flipchart (or whiteboard or laptop projector), under various headings that seem sensible. Ask the six most useful questions (Kipling's six servants): How? What? Why? When? Where? Who? Ask yourselves if you are asking the right basic questions – for example, not 'How do we make our systems faster?' but 'What do our customers really want?'. We once worked for a ball-bearing manufacturer who made the best ball-bearings in the world. They could not understand why they were losing market share to an inferior product made by the Japanese. Their research told them that, far from requiring a product that lasted forever, their customers thought that the shorter duration ball-bearing would do if it was cheaper. The Japanese packaged their product beautifully rather than wrapping it in an oily piece of paper. This packaging was important to the customer as it not only protected the ball-bearings but also contained useful information. People weren't as knowledgeable about ball-bearings as in the past and needed this support. In addition, over 60 per cent of ball-bearings were sold through wholesalers worldwide. The Japanese packaged ball-bearings stood up to warehouse life much better than our client's and the warehouse customers asked for a discount when buying their somewhat soiled product. Not surprisingly, this did not go down well with the wholesalers. End users wanted a cheaper, albeit inferior product, but one that came with more technical information and looked better packaged. None of these points had received any attention from our client. It cannot be emphasised enough that time spent exploring the problem is critical to finding a solution.

Stage 2: Setting Goal States

Goal states are always thought of as green because they are the action – Go – that you want to achieve. Each problem needs a clear goal state to work towards that is understandable by everyone. Goal states need to be kept as simple as possible, so if the problem is complex you may need to have several of them, making sure that they do not contradict one another. An example of a simple goal state would be, 'To lose weight'. This could be classed as a noble intention (NI) unless you had every intention of making the necessary sacrifices that losing weight entails. Noble intentions are often found in areas where you have little chance of making an impact, like 'To change the culture of the organisation'. Be aware of multiple goal states – usually those with an 'and' in the middle. The aim is to make the goal state as crisp as possible so that you get some doable actions as a result of working it through. Above all, goal states need to be practical. Always start with the word 'To', and keep to twelve words or fewer.

Although goal states should be as simple as possible it is important that you don't close down your options too soon. For example, you might choose as your goal state 'To buy a new car', which appears to follow all our criteria on what a goal state should be, being short and snappy and less than twelve words. However, the word 'new' could be interpreted as brand new or new to you (i.e. second-hand), and the word 'buy' might preclude leasing. These are embedded criteria and limit ideas for the solution. The goal state you really want might be 'To provide a solution to my transport needs'. You may not want a car at all! To have arrived at this goal state the group must have made assumptions about other forms of transport such as public transport or a motor-scooter and perhaps rejected them on criteria of safety factors, convenience and image.

Stage 3: Setting Criteria

Criteria are always red because they are the things stopping every idea from being the right one. They are the questions that have to be asked if the team are to successfully solve the problem. Criteria are the anticipated 'Yes, but ...'s for the ideas you will generate when you go blue. They take two forms:

1. Those the team themselves will want satisfying.

2. Those that are needed to influence the people with the resources (i.e. those to whom you have to put your plan).

For example, if head count is important in your organisation, an idea that necessitates recruitment is unlikely to cross that hurdle and be successful, unless you can fund it from savings.

Even before you start producing any ideas to solve your problem, it is important to set criteria against which you will test them. Imagine that your problem is the Grand National at Aintree, Liverpool – the biggest horse race over fences in the world – and that all your potential ideas are horses which have to get over the fences to be the winner. The fences are the criteria. The best horse or the best idea is the one that jumps them all.

Now you may think that putting red before blue has the potential to stifle creativity and will cramp your style and hamper all the ideas that are waiting to bubble out. Many people are worried about this and question the point of appearing to censor the group before it has begun. Our experience is that getting the criteria out has little effect on the generation of ideas. However, it does satisfy for a while those members of your team who think that the whole process is a farce and are dying to tell you what all the constraints are. This gives them an opportunity to do so and satisfies their sense of censorship. Once they have had their say, they are usually content to remain silent, or even chip in an idea or two, having performed a useful service. The alternative is individuals making judgements after all your ideas are out, with no criteria. In this case people will be thinking in terms of their planets as we discussed in Chapter 3. This 'closing down' process is very important to problem-solving, but it has to be undertaken in the appropriate place and unfortunately the people who are good at it have a tendency to stop everyone else from doing what they are good at (e.g. producing workable ideas).

How do you determine the criteria? Let's take our original goal state of 'To lose weight'. What are the things that you don't want to happen while you are achieving your objective? Suggestions might be (a) that you don't want to damage your health, (b) that you don't want to take up smoking as an aid and (c) that you don't want to feel hungry. Any idea that is put forward to solve the problem of losing weight has to fulfil these criteria. It has to have the ability to cope with these limitations.

Many ideas when faced with a criterion can be answered by a straight 'yes' or 'no'. However, sometimes a simple 'yes' or 'no' might not be very useful. You may have to develop a weighting system (nothing to do with losing weight!). Such a weighting system can be very helpful in preventing the criteria being too all-embracing. Let us imagine that you have set yourself the goal state of 'To buy a new car' and that this really is the problem you want to solve (see above). Nearly everyone has done this at one time or another. The first question is whether this means a new car that is brand new with no previous owners or a second-hand car that is nevertheless new to you. Sometimes when this exercise is done in a group different people have different ideas of what is meant, as we have shown in the 'new' example above, and would immediately be solving different problems if left to their own devices.

As it is, you would discover, if you used this example, that people do come up with a level of vagueness that they are happy with. For example, they would say that they would like good reliability, safety features and security. They know exactly what they mean by this and in their mind's eye they envisage a car that is low on breakdowns and faults, with a four star or above Euro NCAP crash test and a marque associated with low amounts of theft from and theft of. However, they are rarely as detailed as this when asked, and need to be pinned down very specifically as to what they have in mind. This is where the example given rather falls down as hardly anyone buys a car in a group. However, it does make the point that the criteria need to be agreed upon and that they need to be very specific if you are to succeed in solving the problem.

You may decide to give all your criteria the same weighting, thereby indicating that they are all of the same importance. This might be 10. All your ideas have to be scored out of 10 in terms of the criteria. Prepare a matrix with your 'ideas' – that is, the several cars that you have in mind down the left-hand side (A to E) with your criteria across the top (V to Z) (Figure 11). You can now fill in the grid showing that car A was best at criterion X and car C at criterion Y, and so on. Car A is the 'winner'.

criteria	V	W	X	Y	Z	Total
Car A	7	4	9	6	6	32
Car B	4	5	7	7	6	29
Car C	4	3	5	8	5	25
Car D	3	6	5	6	2	22
Car E	6	5	2	5	3	21

Figure 11. Scoring the criteria

In this case there was an obvious winner, but had two cars come to the same overall score by diverse routes you would be in a dilemma. Which car would win? This happened on a programme we were running several years ago when a group used this exercise to find a car for one of their number within a fixed budget. In the end it came down to the choice between a brand new Volkswagon GTI and a second-hand Mercedes 280CE. There was nothing to choose between them in terms of the total, although they scored differently on different criteria such as running costs. However, the group had not been entirely honest with themselves. They had omitted to include that criterion which involves what the car said about the person concerned – in other words the criterion of status. After all, isn't that what a lot of cars are chosen for? When they finally realised this, the Mercedes won hands down. The point here is that you have to be very honest and comprehensive about the criteria you choose.

Ask yourselves if all the criteria carry the same weight. Would you rather have a safe car or a reliable car? Give all the criteria a weighting. In this case perhaps criterion X is worth 2, while criterion Z is worth 5, and so on. By multiplying the weighting against how many, out of 10, you think the cars score on your criteria and you will get a more differentiated result. Indeed one of the other cars might come out the winner. See Figure 12, where Car B has emerged as the winner.

criteria					
V x 8	W x 6	X x 2	Y x 9	Z x 5	Total
Car A	7	4	9	6	6	164
Car B	4	5	7	7	6	169
Car C	4	3	5	8	5	157
Car D	3	6	5	6	2	134
Car E	6	5	2	5	3	142

Figure 12. Weighting the criteria

All these examples work well if you have thought clearly and agreed on what you want. They do not work so well if you are vague and woolly. This is a metaphor for the diversity of problem-solving.

Everyone has a vague idea of what they want and very clear ideas about what they don't want. Time spent discussing criteria, even if it appears to be time-consuming, can reap dividends later. In practice your criteria will include such general terms as 'cost', 'acceptability to senior management', 'time frame to implementation', and 'acceptability to users'. But these are also very vague and need to be sharpened up. Be as specific as possible. They are the means to giving your ideas a 'reality check' later on, anticipating some of the hurdles that might need to be overcome in order to get them implemented. Getting this bit right helps the process and sharpens your thinking considerably.

Stage 4: Generating Ideas

Generating Ideas is blue because ideas are always in the blue sky area before they can be implemented. Below we are going to discuss two quite different ways of generating ideas. One is about Old Ideas, the other is about New Ideas. What do these terms mean?

Old Ideas are those that come from everyone's grid of experience (see Chapter 3 for an explanation of this term). You may like to think of this concept metaphorically as a little ball in a v-shaped rut. These ideas need to be pooled because what is an old idea to one person may be a new one to someone else. You may have used them or you may have read about them. Nearly everyone is happy to disgorge solutions of this nature. New Ideas are new to everyone and are usually a fusion across paradigms – a connection of different environments that no one has made before. You might like to think of this as a little ball outside the rut. The New Ideas exercise can make some people uncomfortable and if that is the case do not force anyone to do it. People can learn to do it because there is a technique to it like taking exams. However, if it is not an individual's natural style they will be using coping behaviour, which is wasteful of energy.

These are different from the brainstorming exercises that you may be familiar with because they are structured for results. However, there are basic rules, as in all brainstorming techniques. No idea must be censored either by someone saying it won't work or by the person with the pen just ignoring it. If the ideas are coming thick and fast you may need to have two people writing them down.

The only criterion for an idea is that it must work! For example, if your goal state was 'To reduce traffic accidents', an idea that would certainly do so would be to subject everyone who had an accident to capital punishment. This would not only get rid of the person who caused the accident, thereby preventing them from having another one, but would also act as a deterrent to all other users. It would certainly work. Whether or not it would satisfy your other criteria would remain to be seen! It would probably get rid of all traffic. Another idea which would prevent accidents occurring would be to strap a real person to the front bumper before you set off. We will explain how you get from these apparently mad ideas to ones that will work, later in the text.

The other important feature of this type of brainstorming is to have your goal state visible at all times in green (even if you have to keep writing it). This keeps people focused and stops them going off track and asking, 'What are we doing?' – which we have seen happen innumerable times in syndicate groups.

Technique for Old Ideas – Help/Hinder

Use a whiteboard or two sheets of flipchart paper placed horizontally on the wall or a projected spreadsheet. Although flipcharts or whiteboards may seem rather antiquated technology they are useful in providing a focus around which everyone can stand. Always prepare plenty of these in advance even if you do not use them. There is nothing worse than having to stop in mid creative flow for the paperwork to be prepared, and if the ideas are written any old how they may be lost. One of the problems with brainstorming is that often the person transcribing the ideas was not in attendance at the session and many good ideas got lost. Even if you cannot project a spreadsheet from a laptop it is always useful to have one person recording everything that goes on to the flipchart. For one thing, it means that you do not have to carry all the pieces of paper back to an assembled plenary if you are working in several groups. Secondly, it gets over the transcription problem. It is a case not of either/or, but of both.

Divide the space into four equal parts with three vertical lines, starting from the left, as follows in Figure 13:

Figure 13. Preparing for Help/Hinder

We'll take the example of 'To lose weight'. Always start with the 'Help' column. What 'big' ideas would help you? Think of four or five big ideas such as 'diet', 'exercise', 'lifestyle' and 'nutrition'. These are all ideas that will help you. Leave a gap between each idea big enough to write several smaller ideas in the next column. Now turn to those that 'hinder'. A hinder idea might be 'addiction', 'hunger', 'willpower', 'genetic disposition'. Try to avoid just putting the same ideas in each of the Help and Hinder columns. The problem with big ideas is that there is no action in them. You cannot 'do' a diet. You can be 'on' a diet, but as a result of ideas leading to actions, which we now come to in the 'Maximise' column over to the left. The idea of 'diet' makes you think of smaller ideas such as 'join a slimming club', 'understand the meaning of information labelling on food', 'eat more fruit', 'eat less fat'. Now you can turn to the fourth column, 'Minimise'. What can you do to ameliorate the things you don't like doing under 'Addiction'? Can you find reduced-fat chocolate bars and restrict them to one every other day? Could you use chocolate as a reward for when you have lost specific numbers of pounds? And so on. None of this is rocket science but it does put together in a systematic way all the ideas that might lead to useful actions.

This method will make those people on the more adaptive side of your team very happy as it has produced some sensible ideas that they can see the point of. However, you may need to use a different technique to find solutions that no one has thought of before because no one has had the problem before. This technique would be more useful for solving problems where there is greater uncertainty.

Technique for New Ideas – Get Fired

This technique is called 'Get Fired', because that is what would happen to you if you took the ideas to your boss in their raw state (i.e. before you had worked them through the criteria). Some people do not think that 'Get Fired' is a good name as it might give the wrong impression to suggestible people – in which case you can suggest that it is a shortened form of 'Get Fired Up' (i.e. with ideas). The aim is to move from ideas that will solve the problem, but are generally not acceptable, to ideas that are acceptable. Many wild and wacky ideas have a germ of a solution within them, which can be exploited.

It is useful to have someone in charge of the process other than the owner of the problem, although the problem may belong to the group as a whole. Such a leader is required to prepare the paperwork or spreadsheet as previously. If there is an owner of the problem they should prevent themselves from 'yes, but'-ting any of the ideas. Again the goal state must be clearly visible in green. The group generates ten to twenty ideas. In this case, using our example 'To lose weight', you might 'go on a hunger strike', 'chop your arm off', or 'go in for the Roman style of banqueting'. Now bear in mind that all of these are still 'ideas'. They are not suggested actions, so don't get worked up about them. The 'Get Fired' solution does not have to be taken literally, it is simply suggestive of various starting points. All the above would solve the problems but presumably would not be acceptable. Choose two or three of the most interesting or promising ideas that have been generated.

Spend five minutes developing each one of the solutions. Beware of coming up with 'intermediary impossibles' or 'noble intentions'. An intermediary impossible is something which in itself cannot be done. For example, you cannot just 'diet' (abstract), since dieting requires a (concrete) understanding of exactly which foods you're going to cut down on and how. A noble intention is thinking of having the same shape you had at age twenty-one. The aim is to use the starting point as a trigger for coming up with 'potentially practical solutions' (PPSs). If we take the examples above, where would 'going on hunger strike' lead you to? What other ideas does it associate with? It may make you think of abstaining from food or from going on strike against business lunches which you know are a problem for you, or having a vindaloo after the rugby match. What particular food do you want to 'strike out'? What about bread, or cakes and biscuits? In the next example you could do the same with the idea of 'cut off', changing it to 'cut out' and so on.

By making these connections and crossing paradigms you will produce some ideas that you did not get from Help/Hinder, although there will always be some degree of overlap. However, do not be concerned if the 'Get Fired' technique does not provide anything startlingly new. It also acts as an insurance policy that you have got everything possible out of 'Help/Hinder'. What you are looking for all the time are ideas you can take which will solve the problem. This is supposed to be fun, but bear in mind that some people will not enjoy it at all and it may be kinder to excuse their involvement as they only act as a brake on those who do enjoy the process.

You need to consolidate the ideas from both techniques so that there is no duplication. You now have to compare these ideas with your criteria.

Stage 5: Selection of Ideas

Develop a grid with your ideas on the left and the criteria on the top as previously described in Stage 2 on criteria. Run your ideas against the criteria either using a straightforward Yes/No, giving them a score out of ten (Figure 11), or using the weighted criteria (Figure 12). This should give you some winning solutions, that is, ones that have been thoroughly tested against your own criteria and are therefore probably easier to sell to your own organisation.

This is where you may have to be creative in your use of the criteria. In reality your budget constraint criterion may clash with your reliability or maintenance criterion. Say you had a budget of £15,000 but the new Mercedes you had in mind was £20,000. You can't get a new Mercedes for your money. Does it have to be completely new? If the criteria are revisited perhaps a one-year-old Mercedes with a warranty from a franchised dealer would be acceptable?

Stage 6: Implementation/Action

So far, all you have is ideas. You now have to turn them into actions. This is where many teams fail. They spend a long time discussing what they want to do but they are too 'busy' to take the necessary action to change. If generating the ideas is a strength of your group this might explain why nothing ever gets done! The ideas generators may rest on their laurels thinking that their job is done and that there are too few people to carry out the actions! Everyone needs to be utilised to make things happen!

One solution is to 'marry' an action to a person. Once married to an action, that person is responsible and accountable for it. Every action should be married to someone in the team. Appoint one person whose job it is to follow up on all the actions and check whether or not they are happening. This role is best performed by a person with a more adaptive style (see Chapter 3), as they will enjoy the detail and the follow-through. Arrange the diary so that everyone meets together regularly to discuss progress and problems that have arisen. Many problem solutions fail because there are no diary dates planned. It is a good idea to make them at a regular time, like the first Monday in the month, so that they are easily memorable. If you cannot afford this investment in making the ideas happen you may ask yourself whether the problem was important in the first place. Why have you spent this length of time discussing it?

To conclude, this technique does need practice and it is important to follow a few golden rules. Be clear about what you are trying to achieve and discuss what you all think the problem is before plunging in. That will save you a whole lot of time as everyone will be correctly focused. Keep the goal state up front. Do not force people into using techniques with which they are uncomfortable – there are techniques for all creative styles.

Other techniques for encouraging ideas

We are being very careful here and not suggesting other techniques for being creative. However, it is true that if your team generates lots of ideas to choose from and some of them cross paradigms then you are going to be able to solve a more diverse range of problems. It may be that you have a team made up completely of people with more adaptive styles. It may be that you want to encourage them to produce more ideas and ideas that are outside the safe and predictable. If that is the case, then we offer a few ideas below for how you might do this, but you must bear in mind that your team members will be using coping behaviour and will only have a limited amount of energy with which to do it. This is a big investment of energy on your part and has to be worth the effort.

The first idea we have is called 'Uses of a brick'. Say that everyone has a minute to think of all the uses to which you could put a brick. They will probably come up with ideas like 'a doorstop', 'a pencil tidy' (if it has holes in it), 'useful for writing or drawing', or 'to add to your height' (e.g. to kiss a taller person).

All these ideas are pretty predictable, because when you mention a brick to people in this context they usually think of a straightforward house brick. However, depending on the type of people you have in your team, some people just might come up with the idea of eating and drinking, a description of a stupid person or a person who is particularly kind, or a brick as jewellery. Before we come up with an explanation for these let's just explore what might have gone on in some people's minds and think how you can duplicate the process. When faced with this question, no matter what the item is (a paperclip is another example) people see it first as a literal item rather than as a metaphor, so the first thing you have to wean them off is a literal idea of a brick. Some people cannot think even in terms of parts of bricks (e.g. breaking a bit off to draw with), they can only see the actual dimensions. In different part of the world, bricks will be made of different substances – mud for example – so you might get a few ideas based on mud.

What about eating and drinking? If you can wean them off household bricks you may get an 'ice-cream brick', or a 'tea brick'. (Yes, they really do exist and we possess one. They were used as currency along the silk route. You can imagine how much easier it was to carry a compacted brick of tea rather than loose tea. And if you fancied a cuppa you just broke a bit off.) Where does the jewellery come in? What about a 'gold' brick?

So the trick is to think outside the paradigm even if only for a short time. A more advanced stage is to think of the object in terms of a metaphor. We might think of 'thick as a brick' (a stupid person) or a 'real brick' – someone who has done you a good turn. Although these are culturally based it is likely that different cultures will have something similar.

Now try again with a paperclip this time. The opportunity here is to get away from the piece of metal that can open locks and scratch your back. Anything that can be used as a paperclip can be used for other things. Take kissing. Have you ever used your mouth to carry papers with? Wasn't it a handy 'paperclip' on the spur of the moment? Well, your lips can be used for all sorts of things (e.g. kissing). The list is endless.

If you get movement from your team you are beginning to widen their horizons, but the main message is still to play to people's strengths. Another method of generating ideas is to use fruits. You can have your goal state in the usual way. Then you imagine how you would solve it with cherries. For example, you can stone cherries. To 'stone' might have all sorts of connotations. We leave it to your imagination. What might you do with an orange? Peel it, segment it, take the juice, grate off the zest, mix the juices with others, mix the segments with other fruit in a fruit salad, and so on.

Another method of generating ideas is to use cooking terms. If you dissect what 'bake' means, as opposed to 'boil', 'fry', 'roast', 'stew', 'griddle', 'barbecue', 'baste', etc., it will give you all sort of ideas that you can apply to your problem. The possibilities are endless.

Appreciative Inquiry

Another way your team could be creative (i.e. make changes) is by using the ideas of Appreciative Inquiry (AI), a theory and practice for approaching change from a holistic framework, based on the belief that human systems are made and imagined by those who live and work within them. With its focus on the positive, its exploration of individual stories of life-enhancing experiences, its discovery of common themes within those stories, its creation of shared images for a preferred future and its practical methods of making that future happen, this might be the way that your team makes its own future.[7] This approach enables all your team to use their different styles of creativity to good effect. No one is left with the feeling that they are not creative as everyone has ideas about what they would like the future to look like that emerge from the common themes from the life-giving forces.

Summary

What we have attempted to do in this chapter is convince you that everyone is creative, but with a different style, and that what people often do is confuse style with ability. As this nearly always involves outcomes, who is the best person to judge what is 'creative'? As everyone manages to cope with change and makes changes in their own life so they have a style of creativity which is appropriate for some types of problem. Much distress is caused by labelling some people creative and not others, not only for those so labelled but also for those who are trying to make changes and who discover that the so-called 'creative' types have lost interest before the changes have been sufficiently carried through.

We have introduced you to the Colour Spectrum approach to tackling problems and suggested ways in which you can use it which would suit your team, no matter what its make-up is. Although people can learn a style of creativity that is different from their own it is most likely to be a short-term coping strategy and is generally wasteful of energy and resource. Playing to people's strengths is much more productive. In addition you have the satisfaction of knowing that not only have you valued everyone in your team for their part in the problem-solving process but have used all the resources available to you.

In the next chapter we examine the power of team role. How much does personality affect the role an individual plays in a team and how many roles are needed to make a team effective?

What can you do about the power of creativity?

- You can reassure everyone in your team that everyone is creative and that all styles of creativity are important in solving problems.

- If creativity stems from wanting to improve things, ask the members of your team what they feel strongly about and what is within your, and their, power to change.

- You can think about the Colour Spectrum model in terms of the strengths and weakness of your team.

- You can work through the Colour Spectrum model with your team on an issue, problem or opportunity that you have.

- You can take parts of the Colour Spectrum model – 'Get Fired' and 'Help/Hinder' – and work through these with your team.

- You can become accredited to use the KAI (www.ukinfo@kaicentre.com) and use it with your team.

- You can get better acquainted with the ideas of Appreciative Inquiry and see whether it would work for your team.

- You can use us to help you – mail@devapartner.com.

Notes

[1] Koestler, A. (1967) *The Act of Creation* (New York: Dell).

[2] Evans, R. and Russell, P. (1989) *The Creative Manager* (London: Unwin Hyman).

[3] Kirton, M. J. (ed.) (1994) *Adaptors and Innovators: Styles of Creativity and Problem-Solving* (London: Routledge), rev. pbk edn.

[4] ibid.

[5] de Bono, E. (1985) *Six Thinking Hats* (Boston, MA: Little, Brown).

[6] Russell, P. (1979) *The Brain Book* (New York: Plume).

[7] Watkins, J. M. and Mohr, B. J. (2001) *Appreciative Inquiry* (San Francisco, CA: Jossey-Bass/Pfeiffer).

5

The Power of Team Role

Introduction

This chapter is about the power of team role and how the different team role preferences of the individuals in a team can both help and hinder the effectiveness of the team's problem-solving. Team role preference is predicated on personality traits. Knowing the team role that you normally adopt and understanding how it relates to others in the team, in addition to helping you to understand where in the team's work you can make a particular contribution, can make a difference to the smooth running of the team and affect its ability to achieve its task of solving problems. In this chapter we will explore what team role preference means, how the concept began, and focus on one specific team role system.

Early work on team roles

There are now many types of team role systems in existence. Indeed, you or your organisation may already use one. Such questionnaires are now commonplace. It is therefore difficult to explain what a breakthrough it was when Dr Meredith Belbin produced the first systematic research on this subject back in the 1980s. It is probable that of all the systems his is the best-known and, as his literature says, 'synonymous with team-building', although there are many other systems to choose from. In many ways it doesn't matter which one you choose, as long as it suits your purpose, you use it ethically and it creates a dialogue which enables you to discuss team role issues with your team. However, for the purpose of our discussion we are going to concentrate on those devised by Team Management Systems (TMS) Development International Ltd based in York. Before we do that, we just want to say a few words about what team roles are and what function they serve, by looking briefly at the work of Dr Belbin.

As the first person to produce any work on the power of personality in relation to teams, Dr Belbin described team roles as:

> a pattern of behaviour characteristic of the way in which one team member interacts with another where his performance serves to facilitate the progress of the team as a whole'.[1]

Until then, people were differentiated by their function, for example finance, production, marketing and so on, not by how they behaved in terms of their personality – if they were differentiated at all. In fact, Dr Belbin was being rather optimistic in this quote as some roles, of course, have quite a different effect on one another from that of 'facilitating progress'. Before we knew much about team dynamics and roles, conflicts between individuals just used to be described as 'personality clashes'.

We are now so used to work being conducted in teams, of all shapes and sizes, that it is difficult to imagine work-life without them but, as the Foreword to Belbin's book, written in 1981, states,

> 'Corporations have been preoccupied with the qualifications, experience and achievement of *individuals*' [our emphasis].

This meant two things: first, that organisations were looking for the ideal individual, who did not exist, and secondly that there was no consideration of the behaviour of one individual in relation to another. During the 1970s understanding grew that there are many traits which are in themselves mutually exclusive, such as introvert and extrovert. Therefore, no one person could possibly possess the requirements for every role. However, teams of different individuals were more likely to be able to achieve what a single one could not. This led Anthony Jay to write his famous article based on Belbin's work, and call it 'Nobody's perfect – but a team can be'.[2] This described for the first time the roles that Dr Belbin had observed and how they worked.

Team roles

What Dr Belbin's team role research indicated was that eight different *roles* were necessary in a team if the team was to be successful. This didn't require teams to have eight people. One person could have two, or even three, roles, and indeed they often do perform these different roles. Similarly, the team might have more use for one role than another at certain times in its life and might require more than one person to perform that role. Perhaps a project team wouldn't need a Completer/Finisher (a role that involved tidying up loose ends) until near the end of its life, but might need a Chairman/Co-ordinator (a leader to face external threats) at the beginning, who might be replaced by a Shaper (an energetic, internal threat-facing leader) as things got going.

Every leader and manager has to use the system that suits them best and many systems have one advantage over another. However, after many years of working with teams we prefer to use the Margerison-McCann Team Management Profile, which is part of the TMS suite of instruments. We agree with the British Psychological Society when it says:

> The strength of the test, from a practitioner viewpoint, is that the Team Management Profile Questionnaire has high face validity with managers, the narrative profile is easy to read and understand, and the information and feedback guidance material is excellent.[3]

The validity of the questionnaire is an important consideration in whatever psychometric you choose to use. Team members want to feel that this is a fair reflection of themselves. You do not want people arguing over the validity of the instrument, as this detracts from what you are trying to achieve. The validity of any questionnaire should be 0.7 or 0.8.

The Team Management Profile

Dr Charles Margerison and Dr Dick McCann devised their Team Management Profile not only to reflect individual roles but also to show how the roles fit together in a cycle, which covers the work of a successful team. In order to produce this system their research sought answers to pertinent questions such as:

- how you relate with others
- how you gather and use information
- how you make decisions
- how you organise yourself and others.

All team tasks start with getting advice and information about how to begin. Then, moving clockwise around the cycle, something new has to be started, the ideas have to be sold and developed, any outcomes have to be organised and then produced, and then the results have to be inspected and then maintained.

Each segment of the wheel (Figure 14) has its own name and definition:

- Advising – gathering and reporting information.

- Innovating – creating and experimenting with ideas.

- Promoting – exploring and presenting opportunities.

- Developing – assessing and testing the applicability of new approaches.

- Organising – establishing and implementing ways of making things work.

- Producing – concluding and delivering outputs.

- Inspecting – controlling and auditing the working of systems.

- Maintaining – upholding and safeguarding standards and processes.

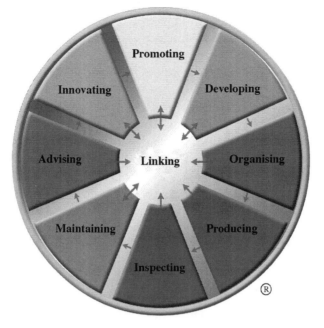

Figure 14. The Margerison-McCann Types of Work model

This is not to suggest that the same amount of time is spent on each team task in every single team – far from it. Depending on the overall purpose of the team, all the individuals in it will spend more time in one area or another. For example, people involved in research and development departments may spend more time in Innovating but they still have a product which they have to sell to senior management to get funding, and they still have to have outcomes if they are to keep their jobs. Those in Marketing are likely to favour the Promoting/Developing segments of the wheel, those in Production the Organising/Producing/Inspecting part, those in HM Revenue and Customs the Inspecting/Maintaining/Advising parts and so on. However, each of these teams needs to cover the other parts of the wheel at some time and in some depth. It may surprise you to know that apart from flying the plane, which comes under Producing, airline pilots spend more time in the Inspecting and Maintaining segments of the wheel than in any other. This may not fit in with our romantic notions of what an airline pilot does, but it is nevertheless true. After the skill of flying the most important role of a pilot is to ensure that the plane is safe. It is absolutely the pilot's responsibility to ensure that it is, before take-off.

As we know, not only organisations but team tasks have a life cycle, especially if they are project teams. What may be required early on in the life of the project may be different from what is required during the middle or later part, and by extension, further round the wheel. Thus a perfect mix for the start of the team task, such as Promoting and Developing, may change to Organising and Producing, and then later still to Inspecting and Maintaining.

Using the Types of Work Model as a basis Margerison and McCann produced the complete Team Management Wheel, which identifies the individual work preferences that relate to the different types of work. Through their research they found that people who share a preference for an activity on the Types of Work Model also tend to share certain behavioural characteristics. Each person has one major role and two related roles. The major role is usually adjacent to the two related roles, making a three-segment sequence, but on occasion, owing to the subtleties of the 200-plus computer-generated profiles, one segment is at the other side of the Wheel, or all three segments are in different parts of the Wheel. The questionnaire used by TMS can be obtained either in hard copy or online, so it is user friendly. It is also in eleven languages, with others in development.

We want to discuss some of the ways in which we have used this material and some of the benefits that teams have experienced as a result. However, before we do that here are brief descriptions of the roles:

- Reporter Adviser – enjoys giving and receiving information.

- Creator Innovator – likes to come up with ideas and different ways of approaching tasks.

- Explorer Promoter – enjoys exploring possibilities and looking for new opportunities.

- Assessor Developer – prefers working where alternatives can be analysed and ideas developed to meet the practical constraints of the organisation.

- Thruster Organiser – likes to push forward and get results.

- Concluder Producer – prefers working in a systematic way to produce work outputs.

- Controller Inspector – enjoys focusing on the detail and controlling aspects of work.

- Upholder Maintainer – likes to uphold standards and values and maintain team excellence.

The roles fit together as follows (Figure 15).

Reproduced by kind permission of TMS Development International Ltd, 2007

Figure 15. The Margerison-McCann Team Management Wheel

You can see that the roles are grouped around Advisers, Explorers, Organisers and Controllers. Individuals in any role may find it difficult to understand the role of someone diametrically opposite to them on the Wheel. Each person who completes the questionnaire receives a 24-page self-development booklet (profile) about their major and related roles and their leadership style, plus other helpful comments about their likely behaviour. We have found that, out of the hundreds of people with whom we have used this questionnaire, almost every one has felt the results booklet to be worthwhile. To obtain more information on this system go to the TMS Development International website.[4]

How we use the TMS wheel

The Team Management Profile is one of our most frequently used psychometrics because it does what it says it does and is user-acceptable. We ask team members to complete the questionnaire in advance. However, before we do this we make sure that they understand why they are completing it and what the purpose of our work together is, either by letter or via a face-to-face meeting. Some people can feel very threatened by questionnaires like this and it is important for them, and for us, to have their fears allayed. Apart from the fact that this is an ethical approach it also ensures that the questionnaires are completed more honestly and that team members do not try to second guess what is expected or required, thus ensuring that we get accurate feedback.

One of the first things we ask a team to do is to look at the Types of Work wheel and try to work out what percentage of their time is spent in each of the segments. We ask them to do this individually and then share their results with the group. Teams usually find this very hard to do as this kind of relationship between all the tasks they perform is not something that has occurred to them before. This in itself is a very important discussion as it means that team members are able to discuss their various grids of experience, the diversity of thinking in the team is revealed, and they also become aware that they are frequently tackling their work from a different perspective. It is also an exercise in listening for the team. How easy or hard is it to take on other people's ideas?

In addition, the team do not always see their work under the headings described in the Wheel, sometimes accusing it of being production-based. This in itself can be helpful as it forces them to analyse the type of work they are doing in a way that is new and is shared by everyone. It leads to a discussion about the role of the team. In fact, the terms and definitions are not particularly production-based – it's just that often people do not see themselves as having a product, even if they do. For example, how many of you were surprised that we indicated that the production of an airline pilot is to get the plane from A to B? You may not have seen it in that way. The results of this exercise are not meant to be scientific, but about getting a discussion going so that diversity can be expressed through that discussion. It is an important part of the internalising process. Quite often, team members vary considerably about the percentages, and that again can be helpful as it enables people to discuss why this might be so and to integrate their differing perceptions. (Bear in mind Chapter 2, where we discussed the different perceptions that people might have about the same issue.) This is particularly true of virtual teams, who often lose sight of what they are producing, *as a team*. They often know what they are producing as individuals, but not being face to face very often the individuals forget that they are part of a team and start to take decisions based purely on their own needs. When every member of the team starts to do this the team soon starts to lose its way.

There is a difference between completing this exercise with a team in which individuals do the same or similar jobs, such as project managers (although they might have quite different views of how it should be done), and a team in which individuals have different functions such as a board of directors. In the former you are asking individuals to describe what is tantamount to their own job because what they do is virtually what the team does. In the latter the team members are seeing the team from the perspective of their own function in it (e.g. as the finance director). Quite often the team members cannot agree on a specific percentage and a range emerges, although this is more likely to happen with a board than with a homogeneous team. As there is room for flexibility within the work of a team we often settle for this, if the spread is not too wide, as it is not usually productive to labour the point and come to a specific agreement.

Having administered the questionnaire we are in a position to compare the aggregation of the team's results, using our own formula, with the team's ideas of the percentages. Our formula is not meant to be statistically rigorous, but it does give us a very good basis on which to get a discussion going about what the gaps are in terms of the roles.

Here is an example of the results from this exercise with a homogeneous team from the oil industry. All the team members did a similar job, although they may have gone about it differently.

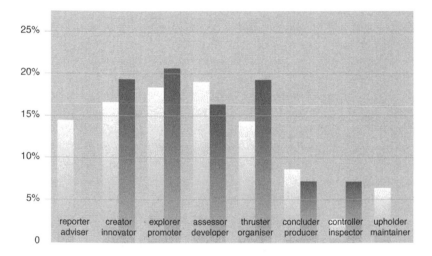

Figure 16. Comparison between required work-types and actual team roles: homogeneous team

In Figure 16 the black bars represent what the team thought was required while the grey tonal bars are the totals percentages for that role of the individuals in the team, according to our formula for determining this. Here it can be seen that this team had a number of members who were Reporter Advisers and Upholder Maintainers but did not see much of a place for this role in their work. By contrast they fell short on several of their other requirements, but not to any great extent. Inspecting is the one area that they looked to have a shortage in, but in fact it would not have been too hard for someone with an Upholder Maintainer profile to cover this role as the make-up of the profile is somewhat similar. There is a possible problem when individuals have roles that are not seen as useful in the team. They might play to their strengths and complete work in those areas which is superfluous to the main task of the team. This analysis might act as a warning to the team leader or indicate to the team members concerned that they might be happier elsewhere.

Figure 17 below is an example of the same exercise completed by a team whose functions were different. Again, the black bars represent the figure they agreed upon, while the grey tonal bars represent the percentage they had in the team according to our formula. Teams often started with a range of percentages. Sometimes it was a question of semantics, sometimes a deeply held view, but, after considerable discussion, they usually ended up with one figure to compare with their preference.

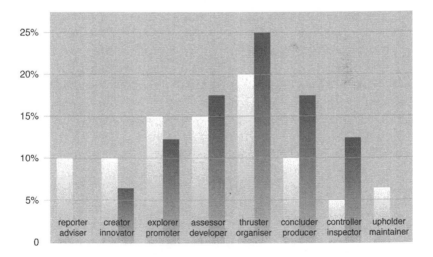

Figure 17. Comparison between required work-types and actual team roles: heterogeneous team

Starting with Reporter Adviser on the left, we can see that, whereas they believed they needed 10 per cent of this role in order to enable them to solve problems, in fact they had no one with a preference for that role in the team. This is not surprising as Reporter Adviser and Upholder Maintainer are under-represented among managers. Although none of them preferred this role, they were able to agree that the person who had Upholder Maintainer could easily take it over.

Moving along, it can be seen that they had 6.5 per cent of Creator Innovator, whereas they felt that they needed 10 per cent. Just a word at this stage about the role of Creator Innovator. In terms of what we have previously said this is both a style and an outcome and is somewhat confusing. However, as not everyone shares our view on creativity and innovation we just have to accept that this is the title TMS have given this role. In terms of personality type it equates with the more innovative style on the KAI continuum.

This team recognised that a dearth of more innovative ideas may have been a weakness for them. They were a team in a new field, faced with big challenges. We were able to work with them to enable the only person with the Creator Innovator role to get their ideas across and for the other members of the team to delay judgement so that they were able to work the ideas through and see the benefits.

Moving on to Explorer Promoter, we find that the team were quite close to the target they had set themselves. For the next three roles they had more than enough and needed to be aware of the dangers of putting too much effort into these roles.

When it came to Controller Inspector they had just slightly too much in the team. However, as our discussion progressed it soon became clear that there were many more rules and regulations in their area of work than they had accounted for, and they felt that they may have underestimated how much of this role they needed. As this was a senior team within the Health Service their decisions affected people's lives, and they recognised that this was an important issue for them. Upholder Maintainer was an area in relation to which the aggregate of their preferences was much smaller than they felt they needed. As we mentioned earlier, however, they were lucky to have any at all. This role comparison engendered a lively debate as to what they were maintaining and was a useful one to have.

Because Reporter Adviser in management is such a rarity, it is often the role with little or no representation. As a result, we often have to coach an individual into understanding what behaviours are inherent in it, if they are given that responsibility.

Figure 18 is an example of a project team. We asked this team to list all their activities by name on a flipchart and then to group them under the headings in the Types of Work wheel, but not who did them. This provoked a lively discussion as people registered surprise at what was done and not done as the list grew. If the descriptions on the Types of Work wheel weren't helpful, we asked them to make their own up so that they internalised the whole process. This exercise often releases a lot of friction and conflict, but this is all to the good, because it is this friction and conflict that is stopping the team performing to its optimum ability. This is particularly true of new teams, although we generally got to work with teams when things had gone wrong rather than at the beginning when it might have been more useful. We have qualified this statement because, conversely, new teams often do not know what they are supposed to be doing and therefore often cannot discuss it at length.

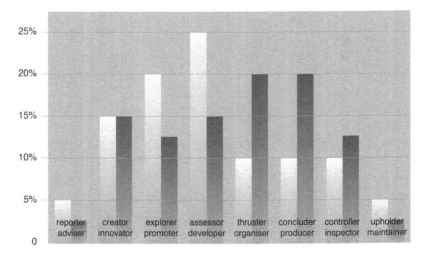

Figure 18. Comparison between required work-types and actual team roles: project team

117

It can be seen that this team were short of Explorer Promoter and Assessor Developer, two roles that they had identified as being important to their task. This was a problem as the team had been put together on the basis of their skills and knowledge and before their team roles were apparent. On this occasion we worked with the team members who were closest to the missing ones and were able to coach them into performing roles that were slightly different from their own.

It is not realistic to expect someone to cover another role by having to move over to the other side of the wheel. However, it is quite reasonable to expect someone with a role adjacent to the one required to stretch themselves to fill it. Sometimes there is no one suitable or willing to cover a specific part of the Team Management wheel. One suggestion we make in this circumstance is that someone from another team should be found to fill the gap. Teams are rarely working in isolation and are often linked in terms of outputs. They either receive the output of another team's work or their output forms the basis of the work of a team further down the chain. Links can be made with other teams who will have future responsibility for a piece of work, and they can often start to maintain that piece of work before it is handed over to them. This often prevents mistakes being made, as there are more interested parties to check that the outputs are what are required by the next team, before they get too far down the line. At management level there are often too many people preferring the Thruster Organiser role.

Sometimes there are a couple of people in a team who create friction or whom the team leader cannot seem to be able to blend into the team. A counselling session with all the parties and their TMS results can often lead to much more clarification and understanding. The TMS creates a language through which people can understand themselves and others. Once this dialogue has begun and there is sufficient goodwill, more effective working can be achieved.

The Types of Work Profile

Sometimes there is a requirement for a more rigorous approach, which is detached and statistically sound. In this case, a more systematic way of performing this task of comparing team task demands with individual work preferences is offered by the Types of Work Profile, which offers a view of the perceived demands of a particular job. However, it is equally important that the results are the basis of a dialogue and not just taken on trust just because they come from completing a questionnaire. The Types of Work Profile questionnaire can be completed by just one person or by multiple raters giving different views of the same job. It is therefore particularly useful where several people are doing similar jobs in a team. The Profile then provides a complete job review system. Research has shown that that in most jobs there are likely to be two or three activities that are crucial to successful performance. Carrying these out effectively can make the difference between high and low performance in a job. (Remember we described the activities that were vital to being a pilot above?) Although it is probably not healthy to have a 100 per cent fit of preferred roles with a job, as this is likely to be far too cosy and not demand any stretch from an individual, at least 60 per cent should match.

Going down this route can provide some illuminating examples of misunderstandings. If a team member is doing a task for 20 per cent of the time and the team leader thinks that it should be 5 per cent, there is going to be conflict between them. If this can be revealed and the actual differences discussed, however, a different picture emerges. These differences can be important when team members feel that they are not being valued by the management and become demotivated. The job may have changed and the team leader may not have been aware of this. Or the team member lacks confidence and requires training or development. Or they are simply using their preferences and what they enjoy doing to the detriment of the job as a whole. Changes can be made to the benefit of all parties.

We used the Types of Work Profile extensively with one of our oil industry IT teams. Within the one team there were three teams operating, each of which had a different job to do, but whose work was interlinked. It was very useful to be able to compare and contrast the roles of the different groups, which were called the Business Information Managers, the Project Team and the Centre of Expertise. The role of each sub-team was different but affected the work of the others. The exercise resulted in several people moving groups as it was clear that they were in the wrong group for their preferred roles (i.e. personality types). As a result they were much happier and their work improved so that the whole team became more effective

Sometimes group sessions are not enough and they need to be backed up with individual coaching sessions. This is because trust among the group members is insufficient for each of them to be totally honest when they are together. This refers back to our Casey model in Chapter 2. The team may need to be a team, but they are operating as a Co-operative Group or even an Uncooperative Group, and trust is low. In fact, we often think that the best way of working with teams is to work with the members both as a team and also as individuals. Sometimes individuals learn some of the things they need to be doing in a one-to-one session which they can then apply in the group. We once had an instance of this where an individual felt that the other team members were not doing what they said they would once they had departed from the group meetings. Partly this was the fault of the team leader, who did not hold the team to their agreements. The team member was able to air his grievances to us in private and we were able to put pressure on the leader and the other team members to conform without him having to suffer for it. As he got more confident, and the others more responsible, he was able to do this for himself.

The QO2 questionnaire

Our final example of a questionnaire looking at team roles is quite different and unusual. It measures the energy people put into either seeing the opportunities at work, or seeing the obstacles. Dr Dick McCann, its inventor, has taken these polarities and named them 'Seeing Obstacles' and 'Seeing Opportunities'. The psychometric as a whole is designed to measure an individual's propensity to overcome problems and have a realistic sense of the issues to be overcome. It's a question of balance. Too much focusing on opportunities may lead to obstacles being ignored and too much focusing on obstacles may lead to opportunities being ignored. The average person at work has a score of 2.2, meaning that they are over twice as likely to focus on opportunities as on obstacles. This points to the fact that human beings are, in general, an optimistic group who think that things will work out. Some people think that this is a biological trait of humans and that we were designed this way as an important principle of evolution.

The QO2 scale is divided into five subscales:

- Multi-Pathways – the extent to which you find ways round obstacles.

- MTG Energy – how much energy you put into 'moving towards goals'.

- Fault-Finding – how good you are at seeing potential obstacles.

- Optimism – the extent to which you can expect positive outcomes.

- Time Focus – a measure of your psychological time and your orientation to the past, present and future.

It is always good to have lots of optimism in a team, as this attribute provides energy to get over the difficult times and keeps the team focused. However, too much optimism in the face of problems may prevent a team from seeing the very real obstacles ahead of them. They may blindly push on, getting deeper and deeper into a situation which may be costly in terms of time and effort and should have been aborted at an early stage. Some Fault-Finding skills would also be useful. Conversely, too much Fault-Finding can stop a team dead in its tracks before it has got off the ground. Obstacles can be seen as just too overwhelming. Some Optimism would be useful. Understanding the balance of these two forces in the team can be very illuminating.

We have tended to use this instrument with teams and on a one-to-one basis, but this has always been with teams we know well where there is a high level of trust (a large OPEN pane in Johari's terms) among the team members. As we have mentioned in Chapter 1, an important issue for you is to determine the level of trust among your team members and how much you can work with them on issues that some team members might feel threatened by. The QO2 is a difficult concept to take on board very quickly. We once had a team where one individual came out with a score of 12 – that is, the results showed that he was twelve times more likely to focus on the Opportunities presented by a situation than on the Obstacles. We made contact with him to check what he felt about this. He was happy. That was how he was. However, we were uncertain as to how this might be received by the rest of the team, which was quite a large one where there was a plenty of camaraderie but we were not sure whether the level of trust could accommodate this result. In the end we did not share the results with the team, but talked about it generally and then gave each person their results. In many teams the results are shared anyway when individuals discuss them in the breaks, but at least in this instance the person concerned had a choice as to how he played his result.

This instrument can be very helpful if there is not much energy in the group, and you need, as the leader, to get a handle on how to get a discussion going on this. Individuals in teams may have very sound reasons why they are not putting their energy into a project. If they come out from this profile as being much more naturally optimistic than they appear to be you will know that something very specific is holding them back. If they are all naturally fault finders, then you must wonder if they are the right people for the job in hand or find other ways to raise the energy level.

Information on this Profile can be obtained from the TMSI website.[5] You would need to be accredited to use it, or buy in help from the organisation itself or from consultants like us.

Summary

We hope we have convinced you in this chapter that the roles individuals have and how these relate to the work of the team are worthy of serious reflection. What we have described above are different ways of looking at the team roles of individuals. Because individuals present different roles according to their personality they will have different effects on the team. Too many with one role and other roles are neglected. Too few with a particular role and a part of the team task may be being neglected. The types of role needed depend on the task the team has. One person can have more than one role. There are several different types of team role systems. Dr Meredith Belbin pioneered the idea of team roles in the 1980s and many people identify with his system. TMS Development International Ltd has developed several colourful and imaginative systems which are generally well-received and can be used for both team and personal development.

In the next chapter we describe the power of values in a team. We ask where they come from and whether all values are good ones. We discuss whether having someone who is very strong on values is helpful or not in terms of the team's effectiveness.

What can you do about the power of team role?

In order to make progress on this aspect of team difference you may have to spend some money and only you can decide how much of an investment you want to make!

- You need to ask yourself whether you think that, from what you know of team roles, you have the best mix for the task you have to perform.

- You could contact TMS Development International Ltd and discuss the various team systems they have, coming to an understanding about which one would be the best for you, the Team Management Profile, the Types of Work Profile or the QO^2.

- You could become accredited in any of the above systems. This would give you another skill which you might be able to use in the rest of your organisation if you were really interested in this work.

- You could use us to help you with your team mail@devapartner.com.

Notes

[1] Belbin, R. M. (1981) *Management Teams: Why They Succeed or Fail* (London: Heinemann).

[2] Jay, A. (1980) 'Nobody's perfect – but a team can be', *Observer Magazine*, 20 Apr.

[3] British Psychological Society (2001) *Review of the Team Management Profile Questionnaire.*

[4] www.tmsdi.com

[5] ibid.

6

The Power of Values

Introduction

This chapter is about the power of values and how the different values held by individuals in a team can both help and hinder the effectiveness of the team's problem-solving. A recent example of the power of team values comes from Ernesto Bertarelli, of the 2003 and 2007 America's Cup winning boat, Alinghi. Alinghi is a made-up name which stands for 'team effort and mutual respect of members' capabilities'. These were qualities that Bertarelli sought as he formed his team. He says that the job interview is the hardest thing a manager does.[1] It is facilitated, he says, when you have a strong culture and shared values, because it is easier to see who fits in with them. 'Your worldview and that of your candidate must be shared,' he emphasises.

However, at this stage it is important to differentiate between individual, team and organisational values. As we shall demonstrate, individuals can hold their own values while still accepting a set of team/organisation values in relation to a specific task or role, providing there is no clash with fundamental beliefs.

What are values and what makes them so powerful? Well, you could say that individuals' values have changed the world – look at Mahatma Gandhi or Nelson Mandela. They valued a certain way of being in the world and put that into practice, thereby affecting millions of other people and how they behave. How does this relate to organisations and to teams? Values in teams are the hidden iceberg, every bit as dramatic as the one that sank the Titanic in 1912. That is not to suggest that values are necessarily an unseen menace. Far from it – values can be an enormous force for good, as we have shown above. However, they can also be a force for evil – think of Stalin and Hitler. Values are also an unseen force because they are seldom discussed, or if they are discussed they are then often imposed from the top. Values are inclined to buckle under pressure. To give an example, IBM had a policy of no redundancies, which they had maintained since they had been founded. In the late 1980s, when the mainframe computer market collapsed, IBM had to reinvent themselves. They had to review all their methods. They had to release some people whose talents did not fit their new focus, thus cutting across their dearly held values. Values have to be revisited at frequent intervals to ensure that they are doing a good job. They are not written on tablets of stone.

As the authors of this chapter, we are conscious that we ourselves are writing from our own grid of experience and from our own value set. When we started business with a group of colleagues we spent a considerable amount of time thinking about our shared values and what they meant to us. These values were then put on our website. However, when a business is rapidly expanding, as ours was, it is difficult to embed values into the culture. We chose a group of consultants to meet client needs. This involved an assumption that the values were shared by all those who worked with us. This was not always the case. We know from our own experience how difficult it is to maintain values. You can read a list of our values in Appendix 1.

When values are articulated and shared they fall into the 'open' pane of Johari's Window (see Chapter 1). However, it often happens that people do not think about their values and they are not obvious to others either, so they are 'unknown' to both parties. Sometimes people understand their own values but are not prepared to share them – they are 'not yet revealed'. (See Figure 1, 'Johari's Window', in Chapter 1, page 18.) Sometimes they are very obvious to others, even though the individuals themselves would be unable to articulate them – they are 'hidden'. In groups and teams people will be problem-solving from one of these positions.

Johari's Window is also relevant in relation to Casey's model in Chapter 2.[2] When you are operating as a co-operative group understanding each other's values may not be useful or applicable, but when you are operating as a team, with real problems of great uncertainty, then an understanding of each other's value system is much more important; in fact it is probably critical for success. Thus it is a matter of investment vis-à-vis return in terms of how much time and effort you want to spend on values.

An example of conflicting values

We once worked for a Primary Care Teaching Trust where the individual directors on the board were all of quite exceptional ability in their own fields. They had been pretty well hand-picked by a new chief executive. However, he felt that they were not working together in such a way as to be producing the level of team behaviour that he had been expecting. He was not getting more than a sum of the parts. They were not applying their individual talents in such a way that it produced better problem-solving and outcomes. Working on values with this team, we found that the director of nursing had a very strong value of teamwork and corporate responsibility and the medical director had a very strong value of individualism and personal responsibility. Both reflected their personalities and the working cultures from which they came. However, when the directors were working together these two values were often in conflict. This created dissonance in the team when it came to problem-solving, as they would approach things in a completely different way from one another. Neither had a language with which to describe the importance of the value to themselves or to the other members of the team.

Their being able to identify and discuss this difference made it easier for them to see where one or the other value needed to be applied to different problems. Sometimes the team approach was important and appropriate and sometimes it was the individual approach. We used the Margerison 'Window on Values' model, which will be described in more detail later in this chapter, to demonstrate to each director where their difference in values originated. The important thing here was not to bemoan the fact that the directors had different personal values but to see different values as providing an opportunity to solve different problems. Below, we start to look at what makes up values and how they can first of all be identified and secondly used, to produce a powerful thrust towards effective team problem-solving.

Where do values come from

Values are born from our most deeply held beliefs, which in turn come from a mixture of nature and nurture – what we were born with, and what happened to us in the early years of our life. Arguments as to which of these two sources is the stronger have raged for a long time and will continue to do so. The research conducted into the so-called Minnesota twins in America makes chilling reading.[3] The research was carried out on identical twins who had been separated at birth and had received different upbringings. The similarities between the grown-up twins in terms of lifestyle, values and behaviour were uncanny. This would seem to indicate that nature holds sway. However, the Jesuits' view that playing a central part in a child's education until the age of seven is critical would also seem to be true.

We have a friend who feels very much for underprivileged people, in particular abused people who cannot seem to get out of a vicious circle of abuse and who, having themselves been abused, in turn abuse others. She feels that they are always labelled as failures and that it is their lack of self-respect that leads them to defend themselves by hurting others. She feels this because she herself had a childhood which was very difficult and she can empathise with how they feel. Her values lead her to an understanding of their condition. Other people cannot understand why it is that, having been abused, you should want to perpetuate that abuse by abusing others. Why cannot such people learn from the way they have been treated? They feel it is difficult to have empathy with people like this. The important thing is that possessing these different values leads to different actions. If people with these two opposing views were working in a Social Services Department, for example, they might behave very differently towards the people who came to see them. That is not to say that they would, because professional training should ensure that their private views were not on show. However, it might in the end become stressful for one or other of the parties to uphold a view which they did not sincerely feel.

Values in individuals at work

It is the behaviours of people at work that concern us in this book. So the big question for this chapter is, 'How do values affect the behaviour of people in teams?' You may recall that in the chapter on problem-solving (Chapter 3) we looked at 'hot spots' and how they affected people's behaviour. We are now developing that argument. Later, in Chapter 9, we will be discussing ethics and showing how different these are from values.

In terms of larger groups, the Quakers[4] and the Mafia have very different values, but they are values just the same. Quaker values incorporate the Peace Pledge against violence, and pacifism, not to mention treating people equally and with dignity.[5] Quakers were instrumental in the fight against slavery in the early nineteenth century and their values led them to do much humane work in prisons (Elizabeth Fry) and to act as mediators between hostile factions. The Mafia, meanwhile, have values concerning trust and secrecy incorporated into their ideas of brotherhood and '*Cosa Nostra*', 'Our Thing'. They esteem the value of loyalty, which most of us would approve of. It is how you put the value into practice that counts. Values in themselves are not necessarily good (or bad) – it depends towards what ends they are put.

You may recall from the previous chapter that there is a team role named 'Upholder Maintainer'. Although this role is relatively rare in managers, people with this role preference can behave in ways that infuriate their fellow team members. On the one hand, they can perform a useful role in the team by acting as the team conscience and making sure that the team completes the tasks it has set itself or the promises that it has made. Alternatively, they can behave as the only team member who thinks that they have any values at all, and as a result their values are imposed on the others. We once worked with such a manager. The members of the leadership team (of which he was a member) made a decision which they agreed not to discuss with their own teams, because of its sensitive nature. However, in his report back to his own team this manager did disclose the decision, much to the discomfort of his peer group. His reason was that his personal value of openness necessitated him overriding his commitment to his peers. He had not, however, shared his problem of conflicting values with his peer group at the time the decision was taken. He led them to believe that he was in agreement with the decision and then undermined them. He was quite sure that he had acted honourably, according to his personal values, because with his own team he had well-articulated team values and with the leadership team there was no such agreement.

Imposing your values on others, without a discussion, can produce problems. A lady we met recently said that 'fairness' was very important to her. She judged everything in terms of whether it was fair or not. Now you may think that this was a noble sentiment, especially in a business context, as she is the finance director of a successful bio-tech company. However, it has very real dangers. She is relying on her own concept of what fairness is, which is not necessarily that held by everyone else. We give an example of 'fairness' in the chapter on national culture (Chapter 7), which demonstrates that French and British views on fairness are diametrically opposed. So how can they both be fair? 'Fairness' is a cultural thing – that is, it is formed by the norms of the group, and dependent on the values of the culture you aspire to.

Another example of fairness crops up in the health service. We were talking recently to a man whose company helps small bio-tech companies market their products. He is totally opposed to the Government's reforms in the area of healthcare. The policy he finds most unfair is that Primary Care Trusts now have the power to determine the type of healthcare they deem to be most important to their demographic area. So if you are in an area where hernias or diabetes are prevalent, the PCT will put money into those specific things. Now you may think that seems very fair. However, if you have a child who suffers from one of a range of mucopolysaccharide diseases (genetic diseases related to lack of an enzyme affecting the sugar molecules), of which there are about 1,200 child and adult sufferers in the UK, and you live in the South-East you will find your child being treated quite differently from a similar child patient living in the North-West. One of the Primary Care Trusts in those Regions funds this expensive treatment and one doesn't, all on the basis of utility value, or how important this medical condition is in its scale of priorities. Now that seems very unfair. Can you have it both ways – both central and area funding? If you have people in teams making these decisions – and they have to – you can see how important it is that they each understand the value system being adopted by other members of the team.

The predictive power of values

Can we ever understand other people's values and how these affect their behaviour? – that is, can we predict what they will do? As Boyatzis, Murphy and Wheeler point out in their comprehensive article,[6] values are a notoriously difficult area in which to predict behaviour. Many people do not reflect on their values and therefore are unaware of them. Others respond in terms of social desirability rather than their true values. If we stopped here and asked you to say what your values were, would you be able to do so? Just to give you an idea of the sort of values that people come up with, we have put a list in Exercise 4 (page 231). Tick the ones that you think you hold and then think about how holding these values affects your behaviour at work. We predict that you will find this quite difficult, and even more so if you did not have a list to start with. If you have ticked more than eight, how do you think you can maintain this number? All these difficulties make it very problematic to construct taxonomies of values and measure individuals. Allport and Vernon are generally credited with beginning the modern search for predictive personal values by constructing a six-category taxonomy.[7] This comprised political, social, economic, theoretical, religious and aesthetic values. Not perhaps a list that we would identify with in the twenty-first century.

Nowadays, Schwartz[8] and Bilsky and Schwartz[9] are the researchers who most writers (including Margerison) make reference to, both in terms of their conceptual definition and of their taxonomy of ten values. Schwartz said that values are concepts or beliefs, pertaining to desirable end states or behaviours, that transcend specific situations, guide selection or evaluation of people, behaviour and events and are ordered by importance relative to other values to form a system of value priorities. His list of ten comprised: universalism, benevolence, tradition, conformity, security, power, achievement, hedonism, simulation and self-direction. Still not words which we might use today in the business context, although universalism will crop up again in the chapter on national culture (Chapter 7). Perhaps an easier definition is Renner's: 'cognitive constructs that explain individual differences in regard to aims in life and behaviour, principles and priorities'.[10] It is behaviour, in terms either of doing or, just as potently, of not doing something, which is the key word in relation to teams.

The idea of values was still in the therapeutic (i.e. curative) domain until McClelland set the ball rolling in industrial psychology by distinguishing the need for power, affiliation and achievement.[11] It was very useful for leaders and managers to know which of these three values their employees had and how they prioritised them. While not strictly values, they were an attempt to explain what motivated people at work. Around the same time (the late 1950s and early 1960s) came Maslow's Hierarchy of Needs,[12] Hertzberg's Hygiene Factors and Motivators[13] and McGregor's Theory X and Theory Y.[14] These were all attempts to foresee the way people would behave at work, and while the latter two indicated how motivated people were, Maslow tried to give more of an understanding of where that motivation came from and what really made people want to work.

Maslow studied the greatest people in history and catalogued what they possessed in terms of personal beliefs that made them great. From this list he produced a list of values which described human beings at their best – truth, goodness, beauty, unity, transcendence, aliveness, uniqueness, perfection, justice, order and simplicity. In contrast to the then prevailing ideas of behaviourism (strictly observational and based solely on measurement, making it soulless and stimuli-based) and Freud (man operating from the unconscious mind and energised by animal instincts) this raised psychology on to a higher and more spiritual level. Maslow saw his hierarchy of needs as a pyramid with man ascending to the higher levels as his needs changed and were met. At the lower level the needs relate to food and shelter, followed by security, self-respect and recognition, until he finally reached what Maslow called self-actualisation. This was a level at which people became truly themselves and became fully functional.

This format was accepted for many years until the work of John Hunt from the London Business School demonstrated that the hierarchy was more like a set of organ pipes, which went up and down depending on what was happening in a person's life.[15] For example, Hunt produced a questionnaire called the Work Interests Schedule, which consistently showed that, following the birth of their first child, men – there were fewer women in the workplace when he was conducting his research – show an increased need for security. He showed that this same need for security occurs when men are made redundant. In other words, people can go up and down the hierarchy rather than ever upward. This questionnaire is a useful tool for establishing an individual's inner world, but is only for use in teams where trust is high. It would certainly be useful to start a team off in thinking about its own approach to certain elements of work.

Meanwhile, Boyatzis *et al.* claim to have solved the problem of prediction between values and behaviour.[16] They propose a model to conceptualise and measure a person's 'operating philosophy'. This assesses a different level of value structure within personality from separate values or clusters of values; it is the evaluative structure within which a person's values exist. Building on major philosophies such as utilitarianism or humanism, the model assumes that a person has a predominant Pragmatic, Intellectual or Human operating philosophy. In a sample of 801 subjects, each of these operating philosophies were found to have significant associations with a variety of the expected behaviours demonstrated in work and graduate school situations, such as initiative and empathy, as well as learning styles, skills and flexibility

Values at work?

Not everyone thinks that their values come to work. Some people believe that you leave them at home. We were working with a group of IT people when a Frenchman said that he simply did not believe that anyone would bring the same values to work that they would use at home. Perhaps this is an issue that should be aired under national culture, but it does indicate that not everyone thinks that they have a role in the workplace. Happily in this case, the rest of the group rounded on this man and disagreed with him. We therefore didn't have to do anything to defend this view, but he was extremely vociferous in his comments. There can certainly be a difference between work values and other values, which exacerbates the problems in trying to identify the former. A paper by Abraham showed that in a study of 165 Israeli managers, life and work values occupied two distinct regions.[17] Health, happiness and love were the most important life values for the sample, while job interest, responsibility and a fair supervisor had the highest rank order in the work values hierarchy, although there is some doubt as to whether these can be called values at all.

There is another aspect to this. Managers do not necessarily bring their values to bear on managerial issues. This was borne out by a study across 22 countries including America, Germany, Australia, China, Malaysia, Canada, and Belgium.[18] The study examined managerial perspectives on corporate environment and social responsibilities. It found that personal values did not have a significant influence on the importance managers and professionals attributed to corporate social responsibilities. Instead, level of economic development proved to be the major contributing factor. As predicted, managers and professionals in more economically developed nations accord relatively higher importance to corporate social responsibilities. Presumably this was because they could afford to. If so, this would be Maslow writ on a very grand scale. Conversely, a study by HSBC Bank has shown that people in developing countries are optimistic about the possibility of affecting climate change (favourably), whereas people in Europe are not.[19]

Our research into team values

Our research into the importance of understanding about values for teams produced some interesting information. In our questionnaire we asked whether people shared their values in teams and whether this led to a team being more effective. While there was a positive correlation between sharing values and effective teams, it was the extra comments which were the most useful. One person remarked that her employer 'did define a set of core values to be followed. However, many people apply their own value systems rather than one defined by management.' She added, 'Management did present their value system; individuals did not discuss these values.' Another said, 'One likes to be able to count on other team members. Different values often surfaced as a lack of trust in others.' And again, 'Differing values may have helped in brainstorming problems in ineffective teams, but individuals failed to recognise this potential and did not explore further.' Another comment was, 'The impact of values on a team was unknown, so why bother?' And finally: 'Most of the negative team dynamics would probably have been minimised if we had shared values.' These comments seem to indicate that knowing or not knowing about values can have a considerable effect on team members. We will discuss some of the issues raised by these comments below

Organisational values

Many organisations have a set of values which they say are applied throughout and adhered to by all. One has to doubt whether members of organisations completely buy in to a set of values to which they have not been a party, but it does work on occasion. For example one might cite The Body Shop as an example where the values of the founder – Dame Anita Roddick – have affected the views of all the people who have worked for the brand, in that they do have a strong shared value against animal testing. In fact, reportedly, it would be difficult to work there without holding these values. In his book *Rethink*, Nigel May Barlow[20] discusses the beliefs of the founder of Lexus, Eiji Todo, which have led to values such as 'Treat the customer as a guest in your own home'. This has led to the delivery of the best customer care in the automobile industry. In this case you have to ask yourself, 'How much does this view owe to a Japanese culture which would be difficult to introduce into an Anglo-Saxon world?' The truly amazing thing is that it is in Britain that Lexus has put such an investment into customer service and it is here that they are treating customers as guests in their own home. Toyota, the parent of Lexus, had such a difficult – some would have said impossible – job in competing in the luxury car market with BMW and Mercedes-Benz that they had to do something quite extraordinary. This was their response and it has been shown to be effective. It indicates that you have to put tremendous investment into company values if you want to make them work for you, but that it can be done.

In 1990, Senge focused on the importance of Vision, Mission and Values and began an explosion of activity in this area[21]. Collectively, the three (Vision, Mission and Values) are known as 'VMV'. We ourselves worked with many organisations on their vision, mission and values but were often disappointed with the poor transfer of words into actions. It's not that people weren't prepared to come away on a two- or three-day course and hammer the What, Why and How? of the business. That was the fairly easy bit. The results were promoted in various forms, including place-mats in the restaurant, but little effort went into winning hearts and minds and changing behaviour. It was the long-term commitment to making them work that was the difficulty. Appendix 2 presents two examples of organisations which see their Vision, Mission and Values as critical to their success. Below, we look at some of the organisations which, from our own experience, put some effort into making the concept work for them. Before we do that we will look at the definitions of Vision, Mission and Values as they are all relevant to this subject.

Vision, Mission and Values

Vision is all about aspirations. These should be big dreams. They are the ideal that we are all aspiring towards. We are moving towards the Vision by what we do in the Mission. There can be one Vision for an organisation with all the substructure (divisions, departments, sections) having Missions that fit into it, or each of the above can have their own Vision and Mission, or a combination of the two. The Vision is the world we are trying to create by what we do. We were recently working with the palliative care team of a Primary Care Trust. They had set themselves a very original and forward-thinking agenda in this difficult area of work. Twenty-one individuals from several disciplines were trying to forge a method of working across departments and directorates and present a joined-up service to their patients. When we asked them what their Vision was we were told that it was all about being very good and delivering the best patient care, etc. We thought that this was more like a Mission than a Vision. What was aspirational about it? What were they dreaming of? Finally they came up with a Vision, which said that they intended to be the Gold Standard against which all other PCT palliative care initiatives and outcomes were judged. This seemed to us to be something really worth working towards and which whenever in doubt about a course of action they could benchmark themselves against.

The Mission is our *raison d'être*. Our reason for existence. What we are actually here to do – our place in the scheme of things. Senge says that core values answer the question, 'How do we want to act, consistent with our mission, along the path toward achieving our vision?'[22] Values do not exist in a vacuum. A team will generally benefit from having a set of values, in that they determine the rules whereby the team will monitor its own behaviour. However, it is much more useful if we can have a set of values which help us towards the Mission and the Vision that we have also set ourselves. As an example, one of our IT project teams had to fit into the company Vision, which concerned the cutting of costs. Their Mission was 'To deliver fit-for-purpose, global infrastructure and operational services, in support of the IT agenda'. The values they chose to support this Mission were 'Trust, Communication, Accountability and Passion'.

Making VMV work for you

A Regional Development Agency was one of the few organisations in our experience which tried to make VMV work hard for them and permeate the whole organisation. Having supported them in the adoption of their Vision, 'Creating a better future for ….. by building a more diversified, self-sustaining economy' and the Mission to sustain it, 'Achieving the vision by delivering continuous regional investment and adding value to it', we then helped them to develop two sets of values, the internal and the external. The internal were a set of values that included 'integrity', 'objectivity', 'customer satisfaction', 'making a contribution' and 'community ownership'. The external values – those that they wanted to use in their everyday behaviours and which could be seen to be working – included 'focused empowerment', 'flexible teamwork', 'openness', 'innovation' and 'managing partnership'. In many ways the latter items were the competencies that they wanted the organisation to be adept in. Having agreed these among themselves the board members now faced the problem of getting them adopted by members of the organisation and making them work.

As it happened, we were also working with them on their management development and training plans. We had already suggested a pincer movement whereby investment was put into a self-development programme, and also a programme for managers which concentrated on those issues that the Board thought were important. Both of these proved to be useful vehicles for propagating the values. The self-development programme specifically related to the values and how an individual could increase their own performance in relation to them. We also ran courses for project teams on specific areas such as team-building. Having helped them towards the basic skills we were able to keep a watching brief on their development. The result was an increase in flexible team-working within the organisation and the completion of some useful projects. The secret lies in making the values come alive and putting the investment into them. Believing that they can be produced by a few and then adopted by the many through the use of a few tablemats and posters amounts to self-deception. Managers have to push to get the organisation's values adopted and maintain that push as people come and go, until they are embedded in the culture.

Another route that this regional agency took was to introduce their values into their performance review system. Review systems should never be static but each year should incorporate some new features that the Board has decided would be a useful feature for the organisation to concentrate on. Clearly these have to be announced a good year before the reviews are to take place and there should always be clarity around measurement and around how the organisation is going to help the individual to achieve an acceptable level of performance.

An example from a logistics company

The attempt at company values described above was good as far as it went, but it was still values imposed from the top with no participation from other parts of the business. An exception to this was our work with a well-established traditional business which reorganised into new divisions. The new CEO took the opportunity to hold a series of workshops for all existing managers, some of whom had been with the business for forty years. The purpose of the workshops was to get managers realigned with the needs of the new business process. They were asked what were the values of the 'old' business in their experience which were relevant to the new business and what was missing. The value of 'loyalty' was now seen in a new light. The loyalty had been to the unions and not to the business. 'Profit', not really a value but an outcome, was seen as necessary because of the shift from public service to an accountable private business. There were several of these workshops, and they were run so that each following workshop was not made aware of the output that had been produced. However, all the workshops produced similar outputs. The workshops gave managers an opportunity to internalise the values and the ability to defend them when they were asked to present them to their staff.

Thus, the points we would make about VMV at company level are (1) that they must be the subject of consultation and (2) that there must be a significant degree of investment in their dissemination before they are understood and adhered to. Turning them into competencies achieves this feat and also helps with the development of competencies within the organisation. To cascade a set of values from top to bottom and make them stick needs considerable investment, resource and maintenance.

Working with teams on values

It is much easier to work with a team on values than it is with an organisation, for obvious reasons. The team is completely accessible and everyone can be involved. Many teams will tell you that they do not have values, but whether it is articulated or not all teams, unless they are completely new, will have a culture which is the result of their 'Form, Storm, Norm' process (see Chapter 2, page 41), and that culture will be based on values in one form or another. The first step is therefore to get the group to articulate what they are. Sometimes teams will come up with outcomes that may not seem like values at all, like 'profitability', but in certain circumstances, as when an organisation is preparing for privatisation (see our example above), this can be a useful reminder of where they are trying to get to. In Appendix 3 we give examples of different types of values for different teams. If the organisation has a Vision and a Mission, the next check is to see whether or not the values put forward really reflect how they are going to move towards achieving that Mission, and in turn, the Vision. If they do not they must be abandoned. You may remember us commenting earlier in this chapter that values in themselves are neutral. It is where they are directed that is important. So in some respects it does not matter too much how precise the values are as long as they fulfil the criterion of supporting the Mission and Vision. There should be a maximum of eight or so values, as more than that is difficult to work towards. They should also be revisited at regular intervals to check that they are still appropriate and doing the job you want – n.b, IBM. In Exercise 5 (page 232) we have written a list to give you a start, but you can just as easily choose your own.

The next step is to get the team to measure where they feel they are on each value and to specify how it is helping towards the Mission/Vision. We do this by a simple Likert scale. Everybody rates from 1 to 10 how well they think the team is doing, and also indicates where on that scale they *should* be. People will vary on how far down the scale they are now and how far up the scale they need to be (see Exercise 6, page 233). The arguments that come up here are a useful part of the exercise and should be listened to carefully, as this is where individual team members usually give examples of what has gone wrong in the past and what they want to rectify. Do not be in a hurry to get to agreement or worry that it is not happening.

The next part of the exercise is to 'fill the gap', that is, to work towards the higher figure. This requires a bit of imagination on the part of the team as to how they might do this. It is often best to start by getting each individual to work on what they themselves need to

140

do to give the values life. Some or all of these can be adopted by the team. We have found it helps for each team member to be responsible for one or more values and how they are being activated. At regular team meetings, one or more team member reports back on infringements or particular examples of where the values have been adhered to. It is a question of investment. If the team takes this aspect of their work together seriously then they have to work at getting it right. It will not happen of its own accord and needs constant reinforcement. This is particularly true where there are changes to the team. For one thing, new members have not participated in the original choice of values and therefore may not feel that they should ally themselves with them. That is why the values have to be addressed annually, preferably at some off-the-job get-together where new members can have a say in any changes. Getting agreement on values is particularly important if you have outsourced or contracted people as part of your team. They may have loyalties to their own company which conflict with those in your company. It is important to try to determine what these are so that you can deal with them at an early stage, and before a team member's behaviour undermines what you are trying to do.

Using The Colour Spectrum

Another method we use involves the Colour Spectrum described at length in Chapter 4, on creativity (see page 87). This model works through a problem from ideas to action. The values are seen as ideas to solve the problem, in this case the achievement of the Mission, which is the goal state. Each idea or value is then subjected to the treatment of 'Help/Hinder' or 'Get Fired', which are useful ways of extracting from the team how they might put the value into practice

Using a questionnaire to determine values

As we mentioned earlier in this chapter, many people are not aware of the values and beliefs that underpin their actions; thus it is not always very useful to ask team members what they are. The answer to this dilemma is sometimes a questionnaire. Questionnaires on values in one form or another have existed since the 1930s and there are various consultancy groups that also do this work. One of the more recently devised questionnaires and one we have used ourselves with good results is Dr Dick McCann's 'Window on Work Values' questionnaire. The format of the profile design has been influenced by the rose window in York Minster, which is where the distributors of the questionnaire are based. The questionnaire is specifically designed to measure the values that are important at work, so there can be no doubt in anyone's mind what is being asked for. The results are based on the two polarities of Organisational Constraint and Organisational Freedom, and Self Focus and Group Focus.

We asked a colleague who also uses this questionnaire frequently what he thought were the main benefits it provides. He implied that the main benefit is that it is a mechanism to explore issues around constraint and freedom, in terms of individual and group responsibility. This not only mirrors the comments we explored in Chapter 2 about why people do not behave well in teams and the work of van der Molen,[23] but also looks forward to the chapter on ethics (Chapter 9). This seems to be at the heart of managing diversity in teams – the balancing of individual needs against the social. Our colleague also said that he encourages people to talk about behaviours and often steers people round to talking about the values that their behaviour implies. He did not think it was the perfect answer to all values issues, and felt that there are some occasions where specific situations such as where there is a 'duty of care' have to be thrashed out in other ways. In our previous story concerning the two members of the PCT team, one preferred individualism while the other preferred collectivism – very clear polarities in terms of the individual and the social.

It is not essential that all team members have the same list of individual values, but they do need to agree on a list of values concerning the work of the team and how it is to be executed. It is also important that the values of the team members are brought out into the open and discussed so that their effects on the team's problems can be gauged. It may be that some values are important in relation to some tasks and some in relation to others. Again, it is the diversity of the values within the team that is important, and how this is handled.

Investing in team values

We began this chapter by quoting from Ernesto Bertarelli, winner of the America's Cup 2007, with Alinghi. He had a lot to lose when choosing his team for his defence of the America's Cup and ensuring that they all had the same values. He also had the luxury of choosing his team himself. However, we can learn from him in terms of winning. Bertarelli wanted to defend his title and win again. He had already proved to himself that his methods worked, and his methods involved investing heavily in team values. If you want to win with your team then the investment that you can put into team values is all worthwhile. You have to keep on investing so that this becomes a way of life for team members. Then your team really will be able to change the world.

Summary

In this chapter we have looked at values from various perspectives: organisation, team and individual. If we start from the individual we realise that all individuals have values whether or not they can articulate them, and that the same value may lead to different behaviours depending on the use to which it is put. Teams need values to enable them to complete their task knowing that everyone is pulling in the same direction. The choice of values should support the team's Mission and Vision. At this level everyone can have an opportunity to make a contribution to the list of values and agree what they should be. Each person needs to take responsibility for one value of the team's choice and guard it effectively. Constant attention and revision is required if the values are to remain alive and useful. At organisation level even more work is required, because in this instance people have not decided on the values but have either had them imposed or, more rarely, have joined the organisation because of what they represent. Here, considerable investment is required. Aligning them to competencies and/or having them part of the performance review system would mean that they are kept alive. They should be revisited regularly to ensure that they are performing a useful function and are worth the investment entailed.

In the next chapter we examine the power of national culture. We ask whether this is a question mainly of chauvinistic stereotyping, or whether it derives from our different cultural beginnings which meant that we had at one time a different approach to life, one based on survival.

What can you do about the power of values?

- Think about your own values. This is difficult and you may need the help of Exercise 5 at the back of the book (page 232), which asks you to choose your top eight values. How do these affect your behaviour at work? Do you have different values at work and at home?

- Obtain a copy of John Hunt's book and try out the Work Interests Schedule for yourself. Think about sharing this with your team.

- If you have already got a set of organisation values, how are you making them work for your team?

- If you have not got a set of team values, what is stopping you having one?

- Think about the values in your team, especially if you have outsourced or contracted members of your team. Is there any conflict here?

- If you already have a set of team values, how are you putting them into practice? Do they fit your Vision and Mission? You might find Exercise 6 helpful in this context (page 233).

- Does your VMV fit in with the organisation?

Notes

[1] *International Herald Tribune* advertisement feature, 11 Jun. 2007.

[2] Casey, D. (1985) 'When is a team not a team?', *Personnel Management*, Jan., pp. 26–9.

[3] Bouchard, T. J. (Jr), Lykken, D. T., McGue, M., Segal, N. L. and Tellegen, A. (1990) 'Sources of human psychological differences: the Minnesota study of twins reared apart', *Science*, vol. 250, no. 4,978, 12 Oct., p. 223.

[4] The Quakers (Religious Society of Friends) is a Protestant sect founded in the seventeenth century in the north of England. It does not have a hierarchy of priests and bishops, but a lay leadership, and is strongly against violence and war. Quaker ideas have spread to many different countries, mostly America and Africa.

[5] Walvin, J. (1997) *The Quakers, Money and Morals* (London: John Murray).

[6] Boyatzis, R. E., Murphy, A. J. and Wheeler J. V. (2000) *Philosophy as a missing link between values and behaviour*, University of Waterhead, Cleveland OH. Retrieved from Google Scholar, July 2005:http://ei.haygroup.com/resources/ Library_articles/Philosophy%20as%20a%20Missing%20Link.pdf

[7] Allport, G. W. and Vernon, P. E. (1931) *A Study of Values* (Boston, MA: Houghton Mifflin).

[8] Schwartz, S. H. (1992) 'Universals in the content and structure of values: theoretical advances and empirical tests in 20 countries', in M. P. Zanna (ed.) *Advances in Experimental Psychology*, Vol. 25 (New York: Academic Press).

[9] Bilsky, W. and Schwartz, S. H. (1994) 'Values and personality', *European Journal of Personality*, vol. 8, pp. 163–81.

[10] Renner, W. (2003) 'Human values: a lexical perspective', *Personality and Individual Differences*, 34.

[11] McClelland, D. C. (1961) *The Achieving Society* (Princeton, NJ: Van Nostrand).

[12] Maslow, A. (1954) *Motivation and Personality* (New York: Harper).

[13] Hertzberg, F. I. (1968) 'One more time, how do you motivate employees?', *Harvard Business Review*, vol. 46, issue 1.

[14] McGregor, D. (1960) *The Human Side of Enterprise* (New York: McGraw-Hill).

[15] Hunt, J. (1986) *Managing People at Work* (New York: McGraw-Hill).

[16] Boyatzis, R. E., Murphy, A. J. and Wheeler J. V. (2000) *Philosophy as a missing link between values and behaviour*, University of Waterhead, Cleveland OH. Retrieved from Google Scholar, July 2005:http://ei.haygroup.com/resources/ Library_articles/Philosophy%20as%20a%20Missing%20Link.pdf

[17] Abraham, D. E. (1999) 'Facets of personal values: a structural analysis of life and work values', *Applied Psychology: An International Review*, vol. 48, issue 1, Jan., p. 73.

[18] Egri, C. P., Ralston, D. A. *et al.* (2004) 'Managerial perspectives on corporate environmental and social responsibilities in 22 countries', *Academy of Management Best Paper Proceedings*.

[19] *International Herald Tribune*, 13 Jul. 2007.

[20] Barlow, N. M. (2006) *Re-think: How To Think Differently* (Chichester: Capstone).

[21] Senge, P. (1993 [1990]) *The Fifth Discipline: The Art and Practice of the Learning Organisation* (London: Century).

[22] ibid.

[23] Van der Molen, P. P. (1994 [1989]) 'Adaption-Innovation and changes in social structure: on the anatomy of catastrophe', in M. J. Kirton (ed.) *Adaptors and Innovators: Styles of Creativity and Problem-solving* (London: Routledge), rev. pbk edn.

7

The Power of National Culture

Introduction

This chapter is about the power of national culture and how the various national cultures of the individuals in a team can both help and hinder the effectiveness of the team's problem-solving.

Culture can generally be described as 'the way we do things around here'. It is as natural as breathing is to animals with lungs, or to fish with gills. National culture is no different. It serves to differentiate one people from another and gives them a sense of identity. One of the best places to observe culture at work is at an airport arrival gate, where passengers are being met by their relatives and friends. The level of noise, the dress, and the use of language all serve to give an indication of where you are.

In this chapter we look at the basis of national culture and ask the question whether or not it really affects individuals in teams and how they behave. We discuss the theories of some of the well-known researchers on the topic and we go on to recount some examples from our own experience, where different cultures have made a difference to problem-solving. One of the dangers of focusing on teams in relation to national culture is that of assuming or presuming that one individual may be representative of his or her culture, whatever that might be. Throughout what follows we appreciate that there is a natural bell-shaped curve to all characteristics, but with much overlap between cultures, with the most difference lying between the polarities or extremes of each curve, which accentuate the differences. We do not seek to be divisive, merely to ask some questions and point to some examples where knowledge and

147

understanding would have been helpful. It is an area that needs more exploration. Should you perhaps be thinking that the existence of culturally diverse workforces is not part of your experience, it is worth reflecting that the 52 victims of the rush-hour terrorist attack on London in July 2005 were from thirteen different countries. This is one of the facts in Ray French's book, *Cross-Cultural Management in Work Organisations*,[1] which develops an argument for national culture and its effects on the workplace being an emerging subject in organisational life.

Looking at cultural difference

How many people in the United Kingdom were a little surprised, not to say quite shocked, to witness the invited guests in St Peter's Square on the occasion of the funeral of Pope John Paul in April 2005 burst into spontaneous applause? In many cultures, clapping shows your appreciation of something well done and is not associated with funerals. However, it is part of the Italian culture to applaud at moments of great emotion, perhaps going back to the roots of 'lauding' (applauding). The more tight-lipped Anglo-Saxons might think this odd while the Latin countries would take it all in their stride. For some years, HSBC bank has been running advertisements showing that there are cultural differences and making the point that these have to be taken into account while doing business with other cultures. A recent ad focuses on numbers that different cultures find lucky or unlucky. You may see this as superstitious – how many people would avoid doing anything important on Friday the thirteenth – but the fact remains that these issues are real to very many people.

Until relatively recently, cultural differences were seen in terms of stereotypes and many people had a list like the following in their office, which purports to pick out the worst national characteristic of each country and was good for a giggle in low moments:

The Multinational employee has:

- The precision of an Italian
- The generosity of a Dutchman

- The humility of a Frenchman
- The charm of a German
- The linguistic ability of an American
- The ready wit of a Scandinavian
- The internationalism of an Englishman
- The diplomacy of an Israeli
- The culture of an Austrian
- The gaiety of a Swiss
- The road manners of a Belgian
- The speed of the Spaniards
- The patience of the Portuguese

What people tend to do is to focus on those characteristics that are most unlike their own, and, indeed, if you take a Gaussian curve of any one item of difference the two ends of the spectrum are bound to be almost polar opposites. But are there any dimensions on which culturally based differences in behaviour can be measured in a way that makes the information useful?

Where does culture come from?

It is generally accepted that differences in culture stem originally from geography, which in turn leads to differences in climate, food, dress, architecture, pace of life, and language, although the latter has some very complex rules and patterns. Religion also plays a large part in how national cultures develop. In hot countries, for example, people move more slowly, dress lightly, eat after the sun has gone down and eat the fruits of the land – such as grapes, olives and figs. If a people were originally forced by their geography to live nomadic lives, they will favour those rules of behaviour which keep their tribe together rather than, perhaps, justice for the individual.

Over time, rules that preserve people become ritualised. For example, the early Indian peoples were nomadic, but as they began to settle on the same piece of land and became farmers rather than herders, it became imperative that they had good harvests from that one place, or else the whole existence of their peoples would be threatened.[2] Placating the gods in these circumstances became more and more important. So did the role of the priests, who saw their

149

powers waning under this new arrangement as the role of the tribal chief to defend territory increased. The chants to the gods had to be done in a particular way, using the same words and sung by the same person, every time, or there would be a danger of forfeiting their favour. This is one interpretation of the Vedic hymns, which were originally part of an oral tradition for thousands of years and were only written down some time later.

In the late nineteenth and early to mid twentieth century there was a great blossoming of anthropology as Western academics spent time with what were then called 'primitive' peoples, trying to understand their culture and why it had developed the way it had. This often meant living with the community concerned, learning their language and eating their food. One such example would be Margaret Mead, with her famous books, including *Coming of Age in Samoa*,[3] which attempted to compare the problems of growing up in societies like Samoa with the problems faced by American teenagers; and Evans-Pritchard, who wrote, among other things, about witchcraft among the Azande peoples.[4] One of us still remembers with what fascination she learnt in the 1960s, from a newly published Evans-Pritchard book, about how the Azande people understood well enough that it was termites that had eaten through the poles, which caused their house to collapse, but were concerned to understand what or who had caused it to happen. To their way of thinking that had to be witchcraft, and they were only too keen to find the perpetrator and placate them. Imagine our interest when, thirty years later, we heard that the same anthropological theories were being put forward to another generation of undergraduates, but that they weren't taken in by any of it. Being African, and black, they had a quite different interpretation from the white lecturer as to what might have been happening. It is interesting to note that nobody took any notice of them. Does that mean that they are still seen as primitive in our terms?

A student of Evans-Pritchard, Dame Mary Douglas, became perhaps the leading British anthropologist of the second half of the twentieth century. She conducted fieldwork with the Lele people of the Kasai region of what was then the Belgian Congo, for whom the pangolin (scaly anteater) was utterly taboo, inedible, dangerous and sacred.[5] One of her maxims was that 'as a social animal, man is a ritual animal' and that Western culture has just as many rituals as any 'primitive people'. Her interest in systems of taboo grew into an attempt to build a typology of cultures based on people's need for classification. She designated two defining forces on cultures as 'Grid' and 'Group'. Grid is the amount of classification that is imposed on people – what they wear or eat, where they live. Group is the force that holds people together. Societies with strong forces of Grid and Group are hierarchical. Weak Grid and weak Group produce free-moving entrepreneurs. Where Grid is weak and Group is strong you find sectarians or enclavists. Enclavists form groups of like-minded friends who reject the rankings, formalities and inequalities of the outside society. Their culture is radical and angry. She suggested that Al-Qaida and its extremist predecessors are examples of enclavists in action.[6]

The implications of this kind of research do not seem to have been recognised by organisations, and perhaps it is difficult to see exactly how they could be helpful to individuals in a team, although they might have been helpful for managers in far-flung outposts. Indeed, there were few instances of teams of mixed cultures until globalisation began to take place in the 1980s. It was not until then that Geert Hofstede,[7] a Belgian, focused on IBM factories and offices in over forty different countries as a basis for his research into cultures. By using one company he was able to keep the variable of organisation at one, and have the different national differences as his other variables. From the data he was able to put together an impressive and rigorous analysis of the cultural differences between nationalities.

Hofstede developed four dimensions on which to measure national difference.[8] Between two of these, Power Distance and Uncertainty Avoidance, there is a continuum ranging from high to low. The dimensions are:

1. *Power Distance.* This dimension measures the equality of power distribution between boss and subordinate. High power distance means that bosses have much more power than their subordinates. Dictatorships prefer high power distance.

2. *Uncertainty Avoidance.* High uncertainty avoidance indicates that the culture likes to try to control the future. It is associated

with dogmatism and authoritarianism, with traditionalism and superstition. The new democracies were higher on this scale in his research than the old democracies.

3. *Individualism and Collectivism.* Venezuela, Colombia and Pakistan are the most collective in their preferred behaviour, while the Anglo-Saxon bloc is highly individualistic. Where individualism is low, people expect more help from family, friends and organisations and give them more commitment in exchange.

4. *Masculinity and Femininity.* Masculinity is related to ambition, the desire to achieve and earn more, whereas its opposite, femininity, is more concerned with interpersonal relationships, the environment and a sense of service. Masculinity prefers quantity of things to quality of life, with men almost always preferring the quantity alternative. (The distinction between masculine and male, and between feminine and female, is very important to bear in mind when it comes to gender difference.)

Another Belgian, Fons Trompenaars,[9] followed up and developed Hofstede's research, using Shell as his organisation. Although a brilliant marketer, Trompenaars is not considered to be such a precise researcher as Hofstede. However, his taxonomy, although complex, is much better known and he has built up a business licensing people to use his ideas. It is interesting to speculate why it should be that the two people who have made the most strides in this area both happen to be Belgian. Belgium has a complicated history and could itself be described as 'artificial' in terms of its borders and nationality, although, in fact, it has had more or less the same borders since the sixteenth century. During its history of over two thousand years the region has almost continuously been occupied by foreign powers, from the Romans to the Spanish, the Austrians, the French, the Dutch and the Germans. It comprises four distinct areas, Flanders in the north where the language is Dutch (actually Flemish, which is slightly different), Wallonia in the south where the language is French, a tiny German-speaking region in the East, and centrally located Brussels, which is officially bilingual. Not so surprising then, with all this background, that people there might want to understand what makes up national characteristics!

Trompenaars' taxonomy comprises seven components. In the following section, we discuss each of these in turn.

Universalism and particularism

Behaviour tends to focus on rules (U) or relationships (P), contacts (U) or understanding (P). Do you get down to business and not waste much time (in your view) (U), or go around the houses and get to know one another (P)?

A classic example of a problem that can differentiate people is that of what an individual would do if asked to help a friend who had transgressed the law. In the Anglo-Saxon world, where Universalism reigns, the law comes first. It is what defines civilisation, and your friend has to pay the price, no matter how sorry you might be to see him or her do so. In the countries where particularism is important – much of the Near, Middle and Far East – what is the point of having friends and family if you cannot rely on them to help you when you need it? It is not a question of morality *per se*. What could be more immoral then letting down a friend and feeding them to the wolves?

Individualism and collectivism

How is the work done? By individuals working on their own and making individual decisions (I), or by groups working together and moving towards compromise and consensus (C).

The image of the 'Lone Ranger' (with or without Tonto), or the man who solves things on his own, like James Bond, is a very good example of individualism. These are the cultures that send one person on missions to other countries as salesmen or negotiators, for example, and expect them to fend for themselves and come out on top. It is very much a Western image and many of our heroes, not to mention heroines, are based on this stereotype. In parts of the East, Japan and Korea for example, the sending of one person would be considered a great insult because this person would be seen as having very little status, signifying that you do not consider the meeting they are attending very important. In addition, decisions are not made by one person alone but by a whole group of people, and time is taken over them.

Ascription and achievement

Is your status determined by birth and inherited status, or by where you went to school and university? Are titles important? Would you challenge the boss in public? Ascriptive status is usually independent of position in the company and therefore has implications beyond work.

Much of the West prides itself on being a meritocracy, where people rise dependent on their own ability and worth. However, going to certain schools or universities can provide an individual with a network that will support them for the rest of their lives, but there has to be something to build on in the first place. Of course, in lots of instances it is not what you know but who you know that counts, and we will never get away from the human trend to further the aims of 'those like us', rather than those 'not like us' (see Chapter 3, where this is developed in more depth). It is interesting to note that although we now use the word 'bureaucracy' in a pejorative way, meaning lots of red tape and paperwork, its original meaning was to indicate that there were rules for everyone and that favour could not be bought. However, in other parts of the world advancement is not by merit *per se* but by criteria such as seniority – what we might call 'Buggins' turn'.

In many cultures age and seniority are very important. An English friend of ours was involved in setting up a laboratory in Morocco. She and her colleagues almost missed their flight back to the UK because they simply couldn't get the Medical Institute's driver to get up and actually drive them to the airport. They were baffled by this until it was realised that the driver had not received permission from his boss, the Professor, and wouldn't go until he had. The Professor was in a meeting, and nobody dared to interrupt his meeting and ask for the requisite permission. This Professor, who was involved in interminable meetings, was also the custodian of the key to the photocopier. Getting something photocopied, especially in an emergency, was very difficult. In the end they managed to get the driver to do most of the photocopying as he spent most of his time waiting for the Professor. Similarly, as the head of the laboratory, our friend was not allowed to do menial, time-filling tasks in the lab – one of the technicians would come and relieve her of them.

Affective and affective neutral

This dimension is about the display of emotion (but not the strength of that feeling). How much do you show you are feeling, or hide, in public?

What shocked a lot of people when Diana, Princess of Wales, died in 1997 was not so much that there was a great outpouring of grief by the British public, but that they were so demonstrative in the way they expressed it. Where was the more usual stiff upper lip? The British were not known for showing any emotion in public, no matter what they might be feeling underneath. Crying in public was not to be expected, and certainly not from men. However, in many Mediterranean countries, and especially those which we might term the Latin states, expressing your feelings loudly was not felt to show any loss of manliness. Quite the reverse. Which brings us neatly to the point we made in the opening paragraph of this chapter, about the spontaneous clapping heard at Pope John Paul's funeral.

Diffuse and specific

This dimension relates to the relative importance of private and public life. It differentiates between a culture or lifestyle in which there is only limited privacy involving a small circle of people (specific) and a culture or lifestyle in which there is an extended privacy zone involving a large number of people (diffuse). Specific cultures will grant much more access to strangers; diffuse cultures grant only limited access to strangers. When these two cultures overlap there may be conflict as to what is public and what is private. Diffuse cultures circle round while specific cultures come straight to the point.

Many British people have now found new homes in Europe – in France and Spain, for example – but how many of them have found that they are welcome into the homes of the native French or Spanish? Many British people and other nationals in these countries, for example the Swiss and Germans, find that they are more likely to live in an enclave of their own people and shop in shops that speak their language, and they are generally not integrated. In Spain, if you are not born in a *barrio* or neighbourhood it is very unlikely that you will be able to participate in fiestas, which are still very largely based on the church and specific district representation. In other words, it is only so far that you are able to integrate, no matter how much you might want to.

In Muslim countries the situation is similar. In the two years during which the friend mentioned above was working in Morocco with her very senior colleagues, they only went to the house of a counterpart once and received an informal invitation to the house of a fellow scientist only once.

Sequential and synchronic

Sequential is about doing things in strict order and one at a time. Synchronic is more about multi-tasking. This dimension concerns past, present and future and how they are viewed. Different cultures look differently at the passage of time and how the future should be treated.

In recent years, a view has been put forward that men can only do one job at a time while women multi-task. Be that as it may, this is about the cultural approach to these issues. How important is queuing to you? It has been described as the most civilised thing that a culture can devise for itself as it is a self-disciplining rule based on the idea of first come, first served.[10] But it is certainly time-consuming. If you are standing in line when a person three in front of you asks for cheese, which is what you want too, how sensible is it for the person serving you to put away the cheese and bring it out again for you when it comes to your turn? Why can't you shout out that you want some cheese too? Because the two people in front of you would regard it as queue-jumping if the server spent time on you before them. In Italy, allowing a mother and child to come to the front of the queue would be considered far more civilised. It is a question of culture.

Internal and external control

This dimension relates to one's attitude to nature and whether or not, or how far, it can be controlled. Is it worthwhile trying to control important natural forces like the weather, or should nature take its course and we accept it the way it comes and do the best we can? Internal cultures favour seeking to impose control; external cultures believe that man is a part of nature and must live in harmony with its laws, directions and forces. In business terms, this will affect planning, objective-setting and attitude to change.

The above comprises a complex set of ideas and is difficult to assimilate without assistance, so let's look at it in a bit more detail. Our aim here is to explore the ideas, get you thinking about these ideas, and prove a case to you that this might be an important area for you, rather than to explain in great detail what the theories are. You can turn to the respective books for that, including for example *Building Cross-Cultural Competence* by Fons Trompenaars and Charles Hampden-Turner.[11] Others that we have found useful include that by Thomas and Inkson,[12] who favour the development of cultural intelligence rather along the lines of the Goleman model,[13] and Olofsson,[14] who offers a detailed account of every country and every situation.[15]

One of the first things to notice about the above list is that the Americans are usually associated with the Lone Ranger approach to business. But that assumes that the White Anglo-Saxon Protestant image of an American is the true one. It isn't. America is now not only the most heterogeneous population in the world. It also has very large, black, Hispanic and Mexican populations and Spanish is rapidly becoming its second language, especially in the South. Things have changed dramatically since Hofstede began his research. America has woken up to its demographic reality and now recognises the need to take ethnicities into account. However, the Americans have always taken the view that immigrants particularly are Americans first and ethnic second. This has acted as a glue internally, but it has sometimes led them to believe that they can behave like that in every other part of the world, with less beneficial results. They have more recognisable brands in the top ten than any other nation, including Coca-Cola and McDonald's. However, when it comes to business, their individualism has been more difficult to export. Having 'employee of the month' in a hotel in America suits the culture, but in many countries in the East pushing yourself forward in this way cuts across many cultural boundaries. Similarly not everyone likes to be called by their first name at work and certainly would feel uncomfortable calling their boss by his or her first name. It would not be respectful. Of course it works both ways. It is much easier to have a team bonus in some Eastern countries than it is in America, where there may be grumbles that certain people do not pull their weight. In countries where it is acceptable the team will discipline itself and accept differences in behaviour, which may be owing to status or age, or another reason which owes its nature to particularism. It is interesting that this has similarities with the 'cavill' debate in the coalmines which is coming up in Chapter 10, on technology. In the mines of Northumberland and Durham this is exactly how the system worked, which broke down under long-wall mining.

It took the West a long time to realise that Japan's working culture of problem-solving consensus and Quality Circles, hailed as the answer to our industrial ills in the 1980s, could not easily be imported into Europe and the United States. It was so deeply embedded in the culture of Japanese life, which revolves around loyalty to the company, as to be almost impossible to replicate. The Japanese word for 'wrong' also means 'different', which gives some indication of its meaning in their culture.

Many studies have suggested important differences in teamwork across cultures, but so far the cross-cultural literature lacks a comprehensive framework for understanding why these differences occur. Gibson and Zellmer-Bruhn have suggested from their researches that there are five different metaphors of teamwork used by different cultures.[16] Analysing the language used by team members from six multinational corporations in four different geographic locations, they established that team members thought in terms of the military, sports, community, family and associates. As a result of this research they felt able to understand the different expectations for behaviours in the team environment. If individuals from different cultures have different expectations of the team (e.g. that it should behave like the family, follow similar ideas to the military's or have aims similar to a sports team's), they are going to behave in a certain way, which may be different from, even in opposition to, that of members who have different unarticulated metaphors. They reinforce the point that this mixture of the metaphoric bases of team performance will affect how the team operates and its outcomes and that collaborating mechanisms are needed to bind the team together, such as a shared understanding of the team's product or strong norms.

Perhaps no one has tried to be more practical about managing people in a cross-cultural context than Terence Jackson of the European School of Management based in Oxford. He suggests, for example, that current approaches to understanding the management of people in Africa are often framed with a pejorative 'developing/ developed' world paradigm which suggests that the African view needs 'developing'.[17] His analysis indicates a difference in perspective between an instrumental view of people as a resource to serve the ends of the organisation and a humanistic view which sees people as having a value in themselves. This 'locus of human value', which in the West sees people as a means to an end and elsewhere as having a value in themselves, has potentially important implications for global human resource management policies and practices.[18]

Scepticism that such differences do really exist remains strong. In the November 2004 Easyjet in-flight magazine, two writers who between them wrote for *The Independent*, *The Sunday Telegraph*, *The Financial Times* and the *Investors Chronicle* argue for and against national characteristics or cultural stereotypes, and are reduced to using amount of alcohol drunk per capita as one of the criteria with which to measure national difference.

Even after the above arguments you may think that the idea that national culture affects behaviour is far-fetched. Time, then, to look at some specific examples.

What do differences in national culture mean in practice?

European management styles have quite different philosophical roots, stemming from how, for example, the UK and France responded to the Enlightenment. The French are rationalists while the British are pragmatists.[19] You cannot get further apart on every dimension than the English and the French, which may account for the antipathy which has existed for so long between the two countries and which Shakespeare commented upon in *Henry V*. As Jeremy Paxman remarks in his book *The English: A Portrait of a People*,[20] anything illicit, immoral and underhand is defined in terms of Frenchness, hence 'French leave', 'French letters' and a 'French kiss', although the nationality in these terms changed depending with whom the English were at war – 'Spanish practices', 'Dutch courage'. In complete contrast to this disdain, parts of France have been colonised by the British, who rave about their wines, cheeses and general way of life.

An example best illustrates the differences between the two cultures in terms of their different approaches. When a leading British packaging company merged with its French competitor, it was an example of two management cultures having to work together, to realise the synergies. The highly intelligent and articulate CEO, a Frenchman, took his top team of twenty-one or so managers into the Moroccan desert for a bonding exercise much enjoyed and appreciated by the international group. When it was suggested by the British human resources director that there was rather more to understanding cultural differences than this, the response was very negative. However, almost immediately cultural differences did emerge between the two groups in terms of how they conducted meetings and approached problem-solving and decision-making. The French did much of their negotiating before they got to a meeting, which they saw as the rubber-stamping moment. The British came to a meeting expecting to discuss and hear other sides of the issue before they made up their minds. The French were very precise numerically when it came to discussing waste or output, the British much more rule-of-thumb.

The UK human resources director had a one-size-fits-all relocation policy which was roughly delineated by company status. That seemed to him to be the fairest way to organise things. His French counterpart personally authorised an individual package for every person who was relocated. He thought that was the fairest way to treat people and that the UK scheme was unfair. The UK director felt that directors had better things to do than personally handle what was to him an administrative issue. All attempts at harmonisation came to naught, starting as they did from such diametrically opposed

160

positions. They never did agree on one policy.

Before too long, many of the original twenty-one managers had left and the company was sold to an American organisation. As a result of this experience the human resources director who had originally requested that the top team undertake some development in cultural awareness realised that his gut instinct had been correct. Although he knew very little of the work of Hofstede and Trompenaars at the time, he is now quite sure that had the team known about their work, much distress could have been avoided. It is from him that this example comes.

All the differences can be explained and understood quite easily by looking at Hofstede and Trompenaars. The definition of fairness depended on, under Hofstede, small power distance and weak uncertainty avoidance (UK), and large power distance and strong uncertainty avoidance (France) – under Trompenaars' scheme, universalist (UK) against particularist (France). Neither of these ways of doing things is better than the other. Each country has an excellent track record in business. They are just different. In fact, if both could learn to pool their different approaches and apply the one that was the most appropriate for the problem being solved, they would be invincible.[21]

There is always an inclination to think that one's own culture is better than another's and to be correspondingly arrogant about it. Nowhere is this clearer than in Africa and India, where the conquering white man has always felt himself to be superior to the 'primitive' black. (See the work of Terence Jackson above.)

To work in South Africa in the early 1990s was to witness the beginnings of a glimmer of understanding on the part of the whole community concerning native culture and the beginnings of an appreciation of the usefulness of diversity. One very senior manager of a very large insurance company told us what a revelation it had been to discover the background to some behaviours he had witnessed which, if he was honest, had greatly annoyed him. One example had been the way a black subordinate, on entering his office, had invariably immediately sat down, without being asked. He had always considered this to be bad manners. But now he was being told that this was a tacit recognition that he was the chief, and to squat down was a sign of respect. It does seem extraordinary that no one had bothered to work out these fundamentals, with the result that they became the causes of discomfort and mistrust between the races.

In general, we Europeans have not taken much notice of the differences between us. There is very little European literature on the subject. Most emanates from America, where real attempts have been made to understand the benefits that difference can bring. One of us recently interviewed a man from a leading armaments manufacturer. He was working on a specific project, and told us that within his team were a Frenchman, a German and a Spaniard. We asked him if the differences in nationalities caused problems that otherwise would not be there. He said that he thought they did. I asked him if he had had any development on the subject of international culture. He laughed. Of course, he hadn't. Does it not seem extraordinary that in an organisation where the nationalities are thrown together no one thinks that anything is to be gained from a basic understanding of the fact that they may differ in their approaches to problem-solving? Is it because it is considered politically incorrect to think that there is any difference at all and that there is a fiction that really we do everything the same way? June 2007 saw an item in the news announcing:

> The Government is poised to give the green light to Britain and France sharing the construction of the next generation of aircraft carriers ... Co-operation between the two countries would lead to significant cost savings on the multi-billion pound programmes. Previously industry executives and defence officials had warned that a joint project would delay building Britain's vessels and complicate the project. However, it is believed that the *possibility* [our italics] of achieving significant cost savings through common procurement, for example, as well as work-share has now shifted the balance in favour of a joint project.[22]

We ourselves have experience from the 1980s of different shipyards working together on projects. There was considerable frustration and wasted effort as different organisational cultures tried to find a way of working together. How much more difficult it will be in the future to add national differences to existing differences among the many organisations already involved. We firmly believe that the projects in question can benefit enormously from having the two nations involved, as each has its own skills to bring to bear. But this cannot happen if potential differences in culture are ignored. They have at least to be articulated and understood by the teams involved, so that no one feels that they are raising difficulties that are not there. To struggle on blindly is to invite a loss of all the projected savings as time and effort leak out in other ways.

The European Union is another case in point. Although this also comes under the area of ethics, there is no doubt that what is considered perfectly acceptable in one country is not in another, with the countries which favour universalism, or the rule of law, having different standards from those countries which favour particularism or those whose people feel that they have the right to employ their dentist or their relatives (who they can trust and who in turn depend on their patronage to be successful) in an administrative role rather than perfect strangers. Why have the EU accounts not been given a clean bill of health for several years, and why are those people who try to blow the whistle on what they see as corruption themselves dismissed for irregularities? These are the different viewpoints that pertain in the EU. How much more so in the wider world. In some cases the difference between countries also means the difference between religions, and this leads inevitably to the differences between, say, Christian and Muslim.

In the West there has been tremendous ignorance of the Muslim world. For example, how many people understood the difference between the Sunni, Shi'ite and Wahabi forms of the religion and what they appear to feel about one another, or about the importance of the Caliphate, before the Iraq War made it only too clear?

What works best in global teams?

Many managers, faced with a team of mixed nationalities, will have been reduced to treating them as they would if they were all nationals from their own country. They will have noted that some things have worked and others have not. Gradually over time they will work out their own *modus operandi* based on trust and greater familiarity. This process can often take several years and there are many mistakes to be made along the way. How much more helpful it would have been if someone had suggested a few simple tips at the beginning. For one thing, would there be a problem of addressing the issue with the team? How often is this done? Asking people whether or not they think that they have national characteristics is not easy. Many people may think that this is asking for trouble. Perhaps everyone should first be asked to do a bit of homework on some simple work by Hofstede and Trompenaars and then be asked to reflect on whether they think it applies to them. We have found that there is some resistance to this at first, as if we are trying to find difference between people. Nearly all consultants quite rightly spend their time in trying to find out what unites people, not the opposite. However, our message is that difference can create strength, so we have to get over this hurdle before we can proceed. Gradually the discussion becomes less personal and people start to raise anecdotes and stories from their own experience to illustrate points of difference. Often they relate to things that went wrong, which is rather helpful to us as it helps to prove that we are on to something and not wasting their time. As we mentioned previously, there is a danger here of loading one poor individual with all the issues of his or her national culture, and it is therefore much better for them to say whether or not they think they behave in a way synonymous with the way their culture might be portrayed. Because it is culture and because of what we said earlier about it being 'the way we do things around here', most people need a bit of coaxing before they can see what they do as anything odd or different from what anyone else does.

Another approach is exemplified by Ernesto Bertorelli in the America's Cup. Alinghi's 36-strong team comprised eleven different nationalities. There, as we described in Chapter 6, Bertorelli has focused on values as a uniting influence. Starting at the recruitment stage he has ensured that all the members of his team share the same values in sailing the boat. On the face of it, this approach may seem to cut across some of the points we have been making about exploring difference and looking for the most appropriate solution. However, without for a moment underestimating Alinghi's feat, we can say that there is nothing very uncertain about sailing a boat, apart, admittedly, from the uncertainty of the wind and weather. Each member of the team has their part to play and, as we said in Chapter 2, there is not a discussion with all the team on strategy and tactics every time the wind changes. The element of uncertainty is limited. In these circumstances a binding principle is the correct approach.

Some practical steps come immediately to mind when one thinks of different cultures in teams, but naturally what you are able to do *outside the team* depends on what your team is there to do. If your team is in marketing or sales then having people on the team with different cultures may help you devise different products for niche markets and a new way of selling them. This is rather reminiscent of what happens in the film *What Women Want* (2000), where the character played by Mel Gibson is given a box by his new female boss containing tights, nail polish and all sorts of female impedimenta with which to try to think up new marketing approaches for women. It really is worth a try. You can build on this idea by asking each member of a culture to bring a box of things that they think represent their culture and discuss it with the rest of the team.

Summary

Is national culture a figment of our imagination or an attempt to sow dissension between peoples who should be able to live happily side by side?

It is neither. Several serious academics have proved that when it comes to taking action, people who live in different places and have different roots will approach problem-solving in different ways depending on what they have found works best for them in the past. Surely that is the clue to how we can best understand these different practices in our current climate. What worked best before is not always what will work best now. We have to examine why we think, feel and act the way we do and ask ourselves whether or not this serves us best now. To do this we have to be able to understand what motivates ourselves and others and ask what behaviour best solves the situation that we now find ourselves in. It is not good enough to stick to national methods and assume that they are the best. Where we have global teams we have the opportunity to pick from a whole range of methods, some of which will be new to us. This requires an investment of time and understanding but where the prize is big enough that investment is more than worth it.

In the next chapter we look at the power of the masculine and feminine, rather than gender. Although we are all either male or female we each contain differing amounts of the masculine and feminine, which affect our behaviour.

What can you do about the power of national culture?

- Conduct an audit of your team members. What nationalities are in your team?

- Ask your team members to talk about their nationality. What difference does it make to them? What differences have they noted between themselves and others. Be very sensitive about this as some members of your team might find this very threatening. Introduce them to the ideas of Hofstede and Trompenaars. The important thing is to look at different approaches in terms of what is the most appropriate in terms of the problems your team faces.

- Ask your team whether they identify with one of Zellmer-Bruhn's research into the metaphors for a team.

- If you have responsibility for Human Resources (HR) in different countries you might look at Terence Jackson's ideas about 'locus of human value'.

- If your team is in marketing in sales how can the different nationalities help you to identify and locate niche markets?

- Try asking each nationality to bring a box of things which they think sums up their culture, rather like in the film *What Women Want*.

- Contact the relevant Hodstede and Trompenaars/Hampden-Turner organisations for more help.

Notes

[1] French, R. (2007) *Cross-Cultural Management in Work Organisations* (London: CIPD).

[2] Keay, J. (2000) *India, A History* (London: HarperCollins).

[3] Mead, M. (1928) *Coming of Age in Samoa* (New York: William Morrow).

[4] Evans-Pritchard, E. E. (1937) *Witchcraft, Oracles and Magic Among the Azande* (London: Faber & Faber).

[5] Douglas, M. (1966) *Purity and Danger: An Analysis of the Concepts of Pollution and Taboo* (London: Routledge).

[6] 'Dame Mary Douglas', obituary, *The Daily Telegraph*, 22 May 2007.

[7] Hofstede, G. (1981) *Culture's Consequences: International Differences in Work-Related Values* (London: Sage).

[8] For further information on Hofstede see www.geert-hofstede.com

[9] Trompenaars, F. (1993) *Riding the Waves of Culture: Understanding Cultural Diversity in Business* (London: Nicholas Brealey).

[10] See http://news.bbc.co.uk/1/hi/education/959380.stm for an item on research into queuing by the University of Northumbria.

[11] Hampden-Turner and Trompenaars, F. (2000) *Building Cross-Cultural Competence* (Chichester: Wiley).

[12] Thomas, D. and Inkson, K. (2004) *Cultural Intelligence* (New York: McGraw Hill).

[13] Goleman, D. (1994) *Emotional Intelligence: Why It Can Matter More than IQ* (New York: Bantam).

[14] Olofsson, G. (2004) *When in Rome or Rio or Riyadh: Cultural Q&As for Successful Business Behavior Around the World* (Boston, MA: Intercultural Press).

[15] For further information see www.7d-culture.nl

[16] Gibson, C. B. and Zellmer-Bruhn, M. E. (2001) 'Metaphors and meaning: an intercultural analysis of the concept of teamwork', *Administrative Science Quarterly*, June.

[17] Jackson, T. (2002) 'Reframing human resource management in Africa: a cross-cultural perspective', *International Journal of Human Resource Management*, vol. 13, issue 7.

[18] Jackson, T. (2004) *International HRM: A Cross-Cultural Approach* (London: Sage).

[19] Lessem, R. and Newbauer, F. (1994) *European Management Systems: Towards Unity out of Cultural Diversity* (London: McGraw-Hill).

[20] Paxman, J. (1999) *The English: A Portrait of a People* (Harmondsworth: Penguin).

[21] Mike Kirkman, notes to MBA students, Durham Business School.

[22] *The Sunday Telegraph*, Business section, 10 Jun. 2007.

8

The Power of Masculine and Feminine

Introduction

This chapter is about the power of the masculine and feminine aspects of individuals in a team and how they can both help and hinder the effectiveness of a team's problem-solving. We are not concerned in this chapter about whether or not women and men are treated equally in the workforce. We want to move the discussion on without detracting in any way from this important topic. Many organisations have policies to deal with equality at work, although there are still some bastions of male chauvinism in many walks of life. Nor is this chapter about a person's sexuality and how it expresses itself. The chapter concerns the essential differences that masculine and feminine genes appear to produce in the mind and, subsequently, in behaviour. Of course this is a highly contentious issue, and as Simon Baron-Cohen explains in the Acknowledgements to his book, *The Essential Difference,* it is only fairly recently that the 'very idea of psychological sex differences' could be addressed.[1]

However, now it seems that it is much more acceptable to look at the differences and indeed have some fun doing so. An item of news on the *BBC News Online* website[2] said, 'Scientists decoding the human genome have discovered that just 78 genes separate men from women. But what are they?' There follows a list of contributions from men and women about what these genes might be and some of them are very funny. What we want to know is how these differences might affect behaviour in teams.

What are masculine and feminine about?

We prefer to think in terms of the masculine or feminine aspects of individuals, rather than their gender. As everyone knows, men can have feminine traits and women can have masculine traits, so simply talking about gender fails to recognise that this is not just about male and female. What we are trying not to do is be guilty of describing stereotypical behaviours, and especially not of pointing out the stereotypical shortcomings, which has been a current preoccupation of some recent authors. We are very upbeat about what the masculine and feminine have to offer the team in terms of their respective approaches to problem-solving. It is a question of understanding what each has to offer and then using that knowledge to solve the appropriate problem. However, it has to be admitted that much research is simply carried out in terms of men and women and we really need to look at this as well, with certain reservations, which we will come to later. What is important to bear in mind is that sometimes behaviour ascribed to women is not necessarily the preserve of all women. That is because it is a feminine characteristic with a normal distribution (i.e. most women will have some, some women will have a lot and some women will have none at all). What is important is that what are traditionally feminine characteristics when expressed in men are not seen as effeminate.

To give you an indication of what we mean, let us tell you about another piece of research which is not about men and women, but about children and the effect of how much testosterone and oestrogen their mothers had in their wombs. According to a study in the *British Journal of Psychology* by Dr Mark Brosnan, head of Psychology at the University of Bath, it is possible to predict how well children will perform in certain exams by measuring the length of their fingers.[3] The study compared the finger lengths of 75 children with their Standardised Assessment (SAT) scores. Children whose 'ring fingers' are as long as their index fingers are more likely to do well in maths, while those with shorter ring fingers are more adept at literacy tests. Apparently testosterone has been argued to promote development of the areas of the brain associated with spatial and mathematical skills. Oestrogen may do the same in the areas associated with verbal ability. A straw poll among our friends and neighbours verified this finding.

Can you do a straw poll in your team to see if this is true? It may have nothing to do with the apparent gender of the person (i.e. it works for both sexes).

What the research says about gender in terms of women and men

The Americans have shown themselves to be the most forward-looking in their approach to this topic. Their demographics have made it essential for them to come to terms with their need for labour and their litigious culture forces them into equal treatment of both sexes. As a result, much of the literature on the subject emanates from America and is still related to gender (i.e. women and men), but it is worth exploring nevertheless. What we will demonstrate later in the text is that many women do have feminine characteristics (not surprisingly, you might think), but also – and this is the important point – many women have strong masculine traits as well.

Litz and Folker have conducted some of the best research on the influence of the feminine.[4] Their research found females to be more participative and democratic, more people-orientated, more likely to use collaboration, and inclined to develop relationally richer networks. They also have a higher preference for using network and team structures and one-to-one interpersonal relationships with their subordinates. The question then poses itself, what happens when male and female managers work together? Do women then bring these skills to bear? One piece of research by Bell *et al.* (from a sample of three hundred large publicly traded forms) indicates that having women (and, incidentally, members of minorities also) on boards of directors correlates positively with the strength of the organisational diversity performance (ODP), which they define as:

> an organisation's performance on a set of broad diversity measures, including the promotion of women, employment of the disabled, innovative family benefits designed for the needs of diverse family situations, progressive gay and lesbian policies and other diversity.[5]

They say their findings suggest that concerted purposeful efforts should be made to increase the numbers of women in CEO and board positions, thereby positively affecting ODP and providing opportunities for competitive advantage. They link competitive advantage to the numbers of women in the workplace but are not specific about what women bring to the task other than this concern for minorities and the underprivileged. What this implies in terms of team problem-solving is that many women are less hidebound by what a person looks like and are more interested in their performance, and willing to take more risks and give people a try. Because it is a feminine trait to build relationships with people rather than see them as machines, they are more likely to spot potential. (This also relates to the work by Terence Jackson on the 'locus of human value'[6] – see Chapter 7 on national cultures.)

Karakowsky *et al.*[7] also discuss the difference mixes of men and women make to teams. They randomly assigned university students to male-dominated, female-dominated and balanced gender teams. Their findings indicate that team gender composition and the gender-orientation of the task can affect member perceptions of the quality of the team's performance, regardless of the actual level of performance achieved. 'Gender-orientation of the task' needs some explanation. It implies that there is women's work and men's work, but the article does not explain whether both genders saw this equally. However, a recent study by Li and Kirkup at the Open University comparing Chinese and British men and women students may shed some light on this issue.[8] Men in both countries were more likely to express the opinion that using computers was a male activity than were women.

According to Karakowsky, teams containing women tend to be more modest and have less belief in their ability. This does not tell us much about what women bring to team performance as these traits can be seen in either a positive or negative light depending on the situation. What it does tell us is that when a group member's gender is congruent with the perceived gender-orientation of the task, the group member will be perceived as possessing greater expertise than a member whose gender is incongruent. In other words, women will be perceived to be better at women's work and men at men's work. This implies that women have to work twice as hard in a man's world, which is something we probably thought we knew anyway (at least the women probably did), but now there is a piece of research to prove it. This will probably accord with the experience of many women who are forging a career in either a very masculine environment (e.g. the City of London or Wall Street) or a very masculine profession (e.g. engineering). This research also agrees with the work of Deborah Tannen, who is quoted in an article by Dr Ellen Weber as stating:

> Since women seek to build rapport they are inclined to play down their expertise rather than display it. Since men value the position of centre stage and the feeling of knowing more, they seek opportunities to gather and disseminate information.[9]

Consideration of masculine and feminine traits is really about appropriateness and sometimes also what is culturally acceptable. What is the best approach for the job in hand? We once worked for a senior team in the Health Service where the CEO was a woman. She had the two leadership styles of Consideration and Facilitation, and was indeed a very nurturing person, who had built her reputation on these feminine traits. At the time we were working with her, her empire was under threat from managers in her peer group with very masculine traits. Having two of these styles was therefore a bit of a luxury if she wanted to survive. She was very reluctant to amend even one of them and subsequently she was swallowed up. Another woman leader we worked with in a very masculine organisation (engineering and exploration), was extremely capable, hard-working and motivated. However, she did have a tendency to cry when under extreme pressure. In other cultures this would have meant nothing (see Chapter 7), but in this organisation the culture was not to show your feelings or emote in any way, and she was subsequently marked down as not being dependable. In such a climate it was a luxury to cry. In another organisation, this would not have been seen as such a handicap.

One recent piece of research by Exeter University for the Chartered Institute of Personnel and Development (CIPD), *Women in the Boardroom: The risks of being at the top*, has found that women are more likely to be appointed in hard times and during periods of poor performance, when board-level appointments are perceived to be more risky.[10] This has been named the 'glass cliff' phenomenon because of its invisible and precarious nature. This has double-edged implications. First of all, these situations can be seen as golden opportunities that might provide career openings for women that otherwise wouldn't be available. On the other hand, the report points out that:

> To be successful, women appointed to these roles have to work harder and better than their male colleagues to retain their jobs because of the riskiness involved.

Because of this 'riskiness' they are also more likely to fail and thus give the impression that they are not up to the job. The research shows that if they succeed they are not necessarily rewarded, nor do they gain access to less risky roles. Further research by PricewaterhouseCoopers shows declining numbers of women working at board level. There appears to be no apparent reason for this, and the 'big corporates' are rightly worried and curious to expose the under-representation of women in the boardroom. If you are a board of directors this may have given you pause for thought and we hope that you will ponder on this research. As a leader of a team, or even as a member of one, you have to be aware of whether or not you are guilty of this particular form of prejudice and try to guard against it, because it may hamper your efforts in enabling your team to work most effectively. As a man, do you demand more from the women on your team in all sorts of hidden ways than you do from the men? We feel that we may have some of the answers to this question in discussing the work of Simon Baron-Cohen, below. We once worked for a senior manager in an oil company, who was very much on the innovative side of the KAI spectrum. We discovered that he was heavily biased against one of the women members of his team and just as equally biased towards another one. The difference seemed to lie in their looks and social skills, a difference that would rarely be counted when it came to men. It was completely unconscious and he was at first disbelieving and then horrified when we gave him examples of his behaviour.

Where research into masculine and feminine behaviour starts to make more sense is in the giving and receiving of feedback. In a later study, Miller and Karakowsky discuss the perceived benefits and costs of feedback seeking.[11] Potential benefits include reduced uncertainty, reduced time needed to complete tasks, enhanced managerial impressions of superior performers, and increased self-esteem when the feedback is positive. All of which should be attractive to team performance. Potential costs can include the effort required to obtain information, perceptions of lack of competence and self-assurance on the part of others, and reduced self-image when the feedback is negative. When seeking feedback individuals experience a conflict between the desire for accurate feedback and the desire to maintain or enhance their ego and image. Women generally are better at asking for feedback than men, and in general poor performers of both sexes tend to avoid diagnostic information. The variables of the feedback situation are complex, depending on numbers and the type of work, but the results indicate that there are differences between men and women in terms of how the feedback process is approached. It is likely that having women in a group will encourage this behaviour and may lead to men actively seeking more feedback. The use of feedback is a very potent weapon in a team's performance and we will be giving examples of using it with our own teams later in this chapter.

Simon Baron-Cohen may not be as famous as his cousin in the world at large, but in the academic circles of Cambridge and the field of psychology he is very well known for his work as director of the Centre into Research on Autism, and for his book, *The Essential Difference*.[12] Baron-Cohen has a theory about the development of autism which is related to gender. He came to prominence with the general public in 2005 when the then President of Harvard, Lawrence H. Summers was taken to task for saying that there were unlikely to be many famous women scientists, which was seen as being overtly sexist. Baron-Cohen came to his defence by pointing out that a supreme feminine characteristic is 'towards empathy' and that a supreme masculine characteristic is 'towards systemising'. His theory in a nutshell is:

> The female brain is predominantly hard-wired for empathy. The male brain is predominantly hard-wired for understanding and building systems.

By 'empathy', he means that ability to feel the pain of others and to suffer with them. It arises out of a desire to care for others. By 'systemising' he means the drive to analyse, explore and construct a system to the point of repetition and obsession. In his view there is a natural distribution of these traits in both men and women, so that a minority of women have very little empathy and a need to understand process, and a minority of men have very little need to understand process and a lot of empathy. Although Baron-Cohen relates this characteristic to gender, he does not have to explain why it happens in terms of its chemistry and therefore avoids the arguments as to what triggers autism or Asperger's and all the discussion around the MRS vaccine. He simply states that this is what his observational research has shown him. His belief is that when a man and a woman with a bias towards process produce a child there is a higher chance that it contains double the quantity of process needs, which leads to its autism (and vice versa). Not surprisingly, there are more autistic males than females, but autistic females certainly do exist and some of them are artistically creative. He describes an Italian artist Lisa Peroni, who had classic autism as a child. She works in a systematic way, producing what appear to be superficially similar flowers, although in reality each comprises a mini-experiment in manipulating one tiny variable. Her technical skill as an artist is extraordinary. The same thing can happen if both parents tend towards the empathetic end of their respective Gaussian curves. You *can* have an extreme female brain, but Baron-Cohen thinks that we may tend to be more sympathetic to this trait and it is not so maladaptive. In other words we probably wouldn't notice or comment on it.

These findings of Simon Baron-Cohen are hugely significant for teams. First, they reinforce all the research which has found women generally to have the empathetic characteristics mentioned in all the research above, namely their eagerness for feedback, their enjoyment of networking and relationships, and their ability to understand people generally. They also go some way towards explaining gender roles. Baron-Cohen says that, given a choice, more men choose to work in 'dominance-orientated' occupations (i.e. those emphasising social hierarchies and control over others), while more women choose to work in 'dominance-attenuating' jobs (i.e. working in a team of equals with others, and/or working with disadvantaged people). (It is interesting that he mentions 'occupations' for men and 'jobs' for women!) They might also explain the findings of Anderson and Sleap,[13] who believed they had identified a bias in the Belbin team roles such that men score more highly as Chairman, Shaper and Plant and women as Team Worker and Resource Investigator. This may not be a bias at all, however, but simply what Belbin observed. Interestingly, though, one of Belbin's examples from Henley Management College where his research was conducted relates to a woman Chairman who was also a fantastic listener![14] They also tell us that many of these characteristics can also, although not equally, be found in men, reinforcing the idea that it is better to refer to masculine and feminine rather than men and women.

Baron-Cohen's findings may also go some way towards explaining the 'glass cliff' phenomenon detailed above. In times of great riskiness you would normally turn to an individual who has good empathising skills, because it is on those occasions that board members are likely to want to capture the hearts and minds of the people in organisations. It is women, as we have seen above, who are more likely (though not exclusively) to embody these skills. (We are not saying that men can't, merely that there is a balance of probabilities.) In times of plenty, people are much more prepared to be told what to do (most probably by a man), because they are prepared to put up with this when such behaviour is balanced against the ensuing rewards. However, when times are bad people need more coaxing to give a bit more for little reward: they need to be treated more as individuals than machines, and they want to know that someone has their interests at heart. In addition, if women are more likely to listen (see below), they might perhaps be capable of picking up solutions among the workforce rather than assuming that they know all the answers. Alternatively, this also makes us aware that women who have the systemising trait behaviour are likely to act more in ways that we might characterise as male, and be even more manly than some men, not in terms of brute force but in their attitude. This was certainly the case in some professions, where you were expected to be 'more like a man than a man'. Now, we realise that in fact some women may well have had more of the masculine trait of 'systemising'.

A feminine characteristic is to love gossip, and this is clearly good for networking and socialising. If you have members of your team who seem to spend inordinate amounts of time at the coffee machine, whether men or women (although they are more likely to be women), then capitalise on it! They might be very useful scouts in terms of your team's relationships with other teams. It is important to know how your team is seen in the company and these team members will be able to tell you. In addition, women would usually be much better at settling down quickly into a new team. In nature, the males are usually the ones who don't move out of their social network and would therefore probably not be as good at getting used to a new team unless they had good empathising skills. So feminine traits in a team are a good integrating factor.

The men who come to mind during this discussion are the real eccentric professor types with very few social skills, such as Professor Higgins in *Pygmalion.*[15] We have all met people like this in teams. They are usually very good at something very process-like, but drive the rest of the team mad by their behaviour in all other ways (i.e. their apparent disregard for the feelings of others and their extreme selfishness). As a team leader or member it is pointless to think you can change or modify their behaviour. Baron-Cohen's theories indicate that these types do not behave in this way in order to create social stress and are possibly just as frustrated by their lack of social skills as are their fellow team members. They simply do not have the wherewithal to be able to function in this way. It is simply the price you may have to pay for having such a member on your team and being able to benefit from their aptitude. What might help is explaining Baron-Cohen's theories to the team and asking them for their extra consideration and sympathy. Once they have understood the implications most team members (and especially those with strong empathising traits) will rally round and use their empathising qualities to smooth over any rough patches.

Research shows that women are better listeners, a trait that is extremely useful to have in a team which is problem-solving. Some of this difference in listening can be explained by the ways in which men are talked to. According to Fran Molloy,[16] Dr Ken Rowe, a research director at the Australian Council for Educational Research, advises speaking slowly, grouping each piece of information into a separate phrase, and maintaining eye contact. A 65-year-old woman, who had heard Rowe's advice over the radio, called to tell him the results of doing what he suggested. After she had caught her husband's attention and spoken slowly in short phrases, her husband told her that it was the first time since they'd been married that he'd ever really understood what she had said to him. Apparently this also works wonders in the classroom. Perhaps if no one seems to listen at meetings in your team you might decide to try this method! There is also evidence of a difference between boys' and girls' hearing from an early age and many women don't show as much sign of hearing loss as early as men do, although some of these differences are explained by men being more likely to have noisy occupations. Further evidence indicates that the difference is caused by physical properties. Dr Leonard Sax cites research into physical differences in the structure of the ear showing girls are born with a shorter and stiffer cochlea than boys, providing a more sensitive frequency response. He also thinks that females have better hearing in the conversational range. The US audiologist John Corso showed in 1959 that females appeared to hear better at higher frequencies. A recent study has reinforced this view that men simply cannot hear women's voices because their ears are not designed to do so. The register of a man's ear covers much deeper notes than the high notes of a woman's voice and so in truth it can be said that he does not hear her when she speaks. The hairs of 'his' inner ear simply do not resonate. Another idea is that men have to 'hear' women in two distinct parts of the brain, involving speech and music, which means using far more energy and brain-power, making it more likely that they will switch off. However, all these later research results should be treated with caution as they are contentious.

When nursing opened its ranks to men in the 1960s in the United Kingdom it was fascinating to see the single-minded way in which men rose in the hierarchy, out of all proportion to their numbers. In a profession which single women had seen as a vocation which substituted for the many aspects of family life from which they were excluded, here was a new breed who saw it as a profession rather than a vocation. The same is now happening in medicine, where half the students are now women, and although most heads of departments are men, you are just as likely to see a woman consultant, especially in fields such as radiology. As bedside manner has become more important and patients can pick and choose, the arrogance of the old male consultant, who always knew best, like Sir Lancelot Spratt in *Doctor At Large*[17] and its successors, has had to give way to the subtler skills of listening and relationships. Of course, this has not happened everywhere and we are not advocating anything other than a meritocracy – we are simply noticing and remarking on the fact that these more empathetic skills are more in demand.

One example of how men and women behave differently, which reinforced much of the research above, came to our attention quite recently. A neighbour of ours is studying for a qualification in animation. At the college she attends, people are divided into groups for projects, the marks for which go towards the degree. As a late entrant to the field of animation and therefore not yet excelling in the kind of advanced computer skills needed, she found herself in a group with three men who had mastered all the techniques. (She herself described them as real computer 'nerds', and as she is married to a computer professional she should be able to recognise one.) Her contribution to the project was to hold the group together by organising them and making sure that there was an output to be marked. Now you may be thinking that was rather good organisation on the part of the college lecturers as they had complementary skills. She, however, was made to feel that her lack of computer skills was a real drawback to the group's work. None of the men was at all sympathetic to the fact that she was new to animation. The rub came when the group was asked to give a score to individuals, based on their contribution, which was to constitute their mark towards the degree. She was given a very low mark by the other three, who had not appreciated her skills. They gave each other high marks. She in turn gave the three men high marks, because she admired what they had been able to achieve. She was also aware that it contributed to the degree and she did not feel that she should mark them down. This might have been misguided, but it did indicate her ability to empathise and feel their pain in the event of a low mark. They obviously had no such feelings. When she complained to the college authorities that without her contribution there would have been nothing to mark, she was given very short shrift. The marks remained and actually affected the level of her degree.

This situation is one that crops up all the time and anyone who has undertaken study for a degree will probably have come across it. What happens is that either people are put into groups and the resulting work is marked by the lecturer or outside body or, as in this case, the group marks itself. In this particular instance we have highlighted the injustice in relation to the masculine and feminine. Just as often, however, the group falls apart because no one gives those involved any help in understanding group dynamics or their own particular team role. It is a 'sink or swim' attitude which is utterly deplorable. Lecturers who do this should think again.

As a male team leader in Britain you may have to get used to working with more women in your team. University admission tutors are concerned about the growing dominance of female students in British universities. A new survey has revealed that in 2006, 47 per cent of 17-to-30-year-old women went into higher education, compared to 37 per cent of young men.[18] This gap originates in the underachievement of boys at school. Girls are leaving boys behind in almost every subject including the traditional 'male' areas. It isn't only in Britain. The same is true in America, and according to Professor Drummond Bone, President of Universities UK, women are in the majority in all university sectors across Europe, except Germany. Perhaps that is why research has indicated that, by 2020, 53 per cent of millionaires in the UK will be women. Women are deriving greater happiness from wealth through their own work, rather than through marriage or inheritance.

If you are a woman team leader, where do you think you lie on the continuum between feminine or masculine? We probably haven't told you anything you didn't know before, merely provided you with some evidence which might on occasion be useful.

Summary

What we have tried to do in this chapter, without for a moment denying the importance of equal opportunities, is to show you that when it comes to working together in teams we should be looking for equal opportunities for both feminine and masculine traits, whatever sex they turn up in. We have also given you evidence that such traits exist. We have rather tended to concentrate on the feminine ones because they are the ones that tend to get overlooked in a business context, but they are now gradually being seen for what they are – different and useful. Again, it is about appropriateness. On some occasions feminine characteristics will be more useful and in others they won't be. Usually it is about the feminine and masculine working together, which is probably why they were designed like that in the first place. There is now little doubt that people with a strong feminine aspect have more empathy, like networking, feedback and being in teams, are somewhat modest and self-deprecating and are good listeners. All these attributes are useful for team working, especially in certain professions and under certain circumstances, but you cannot run teams solely on them. Masculine traits are essential too. However, feminine traits probably have not been utilised sufficiently in the past. Putting these attributes to better use should ensure that the team is more versatile and able to withstand more threats and solve more problems, which is the aim of this book.

In the next chapter we discuss the power of ethics. We ask whether or not they are different from values, or are relevant to teams other than ethics committees, and give some everyday examples of how ethics affect everyone at work.

What can you do about the power of masculine and feminine?

- Are you aware of the masculine and feminine traits around you in your team? Do you tend to favour one or the other, or do you think you give these traits opportunities depending on the problem to be solved?

- Try the finger test with your team. Does it prove or disprove the theory?

- Does having women on your team influence it at all? What ways can you discern? Conversely, is there anything your team does which militates against women and prevents them from contributing?

- Do you encourage your team members to give each other feedback? Do you set an example by doing it yourself?

- Do you encourage the socialisers in your team, of whatever sex, to find out what other teams think of your team? This could lead to your team making more of an impact in the organisation, especially if your standing is currently not very high.

- Do you use feminine traits in situations where more listening is required and there is a need for teamwork and networking?

Notes

[1] Baron-Cohen, S. (2004) *The Essential Difference* (Harmondsworth: Penguin).

[2] Published 19 Jun. 2003.

[3] Holden, C. (2007) 'See those fingers? Do the math', *Science Now*, May.

[4] Litz, R., and Folker, C. (2002) 'When he and she sell seashells: exploring the relationship between management team gender-balance and small firm performance', *Journal of Developmental Entrepreneurship*, vol. 7, no. 4, p. 341.

[5] Bell, M. P., Gilley, K. M. and Coombs, J. (2003) 'Diversity at the top: effects of CEO and board member diversity on organisational diversity', paper presented at the Academy of Management meeting, Seattle.

[6] Jackson, T. (2002) 'Reframing human resource management in Africa: a cross-cultural perspective', *International Journal of Human Resource Management*, vol. 13, issue 7.

[7] Karakowsky, L., McBey, K. and Chuang, Y.-T. (2004) 'Perceptions of team performance: the impact of group composition and task-based cues', *Journal of Managerial Psychology*, vol. 19, issue 5, p. 506.

[8] Li, N. and Kirkup, G. (2007) 'Gender and cultural differences in Internet use: a study of China and the UK', *Computers and Education*, vol. 48, issue 2, Feb.

[9] Weber, E. (2006) 'Now hear this: differences in how men and women listen', *Vegetarian Times*, Nov.

[10] Worman, D. (2007) 'How fair are boardroom affairs?', *Impact: Quarterly Update on CIPD Policy and Research*, issue 19, May.

[11] Miller, Diane, Karakowsky, L. (2005) 'Gender influences as an impediment to knowledge sharing: when men and women fail to seek peer feedback', *Journal of Psychology*, vol. 139, issue 2, pp. 101–18.

[12] Baron-Cohen, S. (2004) *The Essential Difference* (Harmondsworth: Penguin).

[13] Anderson, N. and Sleap, S. (2004) 'An evaluation of gender differences on the Belbin Team Role Self-Perception Inventory', *Journal of Occupational and Organisational Psychology*, vol. 77, issue 3, pp. 429–37.

[14] Belbin, R. M. (1981) *Management Teams: Why They Succeed or Fail* (London: Heinemann)..

[15] George Bernard Shaw, *Pygmalion* (1916).

[16] Malloy, Fran (2006) 'A right earful', *Health and Fitness* (Australia), Jun.

[17] *Doctor at Large* was a 1957 film based on the book by Richard Gordon and starring Dirk Bogarde and James Robertson Justice.

[18] *The Sunday Telegraph*, 8 Jul. 2007.

9

The Power of Ethics

Introduction

This chapter is about the power of ethics and how ethics can both help and hinder the effectiveness of the team's problem-solving, particularly at senior level.

In a previous chapter we discussed the power of values in teams, at some length. The two concepts, values and ethics, are certainly used interchangeably by anybody and everybody who has something to say about them, rather like creativity and innovation. How are ethics different from values? Values are an outcome from deeply held beliefs, and not necessarily all to the good, as we have shown in the previous chapter, while ethics, which are very much related to countries, institutions and organisations, are usually a standard of behaviour that has been agreed as being appropriate. They invariably comprise in this context a corporate set of rules about the way an organisation wants to conduct its business. On the face of it, ethics may not seem to be the sort of issue that affects teams in general, but more the sort of thing that the top brass should be worrying over. This is what you, the reader, might be thinking. They're OK, but how do they affect me? Although this question might be asked in relation to ethics rather more than in relation to the other diversity factors we have discussed so far, we would like to argue that ethics do concern all of us and we can, as groups, decide if we want to condone the taking of drugs in our sports team, the sexual harassment and bullying of our junior typist in the back office, or the mistreatment of old people in a ward. We are all faced with errant behaviour every day of our lives whether we choose to ignore and/or condone it or not. Do you know someone at work who is drinking heavily and driving or is sexually harassing someone who can't defend themselves and are doing nothing about it? Sticking up for what you believe is right can be very tough, as the examples of whistle-blowers we detail below show only too well.

Another fact might set you thinking. According to the accountancy firm BBO Stoy Hayward's *Fraud Track 2006* report, the value of employee fraud rose by almost 80 per cent between 2004 and 2005, and has risen by more than 200 per cent since 2003. Such is the concern that the Chartered Institute of Personnel and Development (CIPD) has issued a report, *Tackling Staff Fraud and Dishonesty*, in conjunction with CIFAS, a not-for-profit fraud prevention service.[1]

Where did it all start?

As we will see further on in this chapter, the Greek philosophers were very exercised by the subject of ethics, and philosophers ever since have been debating the issue. The business world has always been seen to be without much of a conscience by those outside it, and indeed in their eagerness to make money many people in business seem to think that they are above both the law and any moral prohibition. The nineteenth-century English commercial establishment was scandalised by the goings-on in 'lawless' America, (railroads, for example), and indeed when it comes to major business scandals the United States has had more than its fair share, although it is true that media interest in the US ensures a disproportionate amount of coverage, compared to other countries with less media exposure. In India and China, for example, the press is just not as investigative as it is in the West.

Towards the beginning of the 1980s, with conspicuous consumption in full flow, and globalisation having more impact, more interest began to be shown in what was happening within business. Later in that decade, writing in 1987 in the British Airways in-flight magazine, Robert Heller was one of the first management journalists to comment on the subject of ethics, but then as the founding editor of *Management Today* he was always ahead of the game.[2] First of all he asked the question:

> Why should ethics in business be different from those anywhere else?

then continued,

> After all, the ethical businessperson doesn't break the law and does follow the Ten Commandments, as best they may. However, if business competition means anything, it means coveting, if not thy neighbour's ox, his market share, his product line, even his prosperity.

He then went on to talk about an executive of Vicks (of VapoRub fame), now part of the Proctor & Gamble empire, who took prospective managers to a very prestigious venue and posed the following problem. If a supplier approached them out of the blue and offered to undercut their own reliable and genial supplier of twenty years by a large and lucrative margin, what would they do? They had the choice of taking it, giving their original supplier a chance to lower his price, or telling the undercutter to get lost. This problem would cause a lot of debate among prospective managers. The executive would cut through this discussion and baldly state that they would take the lower price. No ifs, no buts. And if they wanted to get into this prestigious venue on their own initiative they had better think like that too. As Heller said, there is a certain logic in this response. Both the workforce and shareholders depend on the company doing well and being as profitable as possible. Thus the issue of business ethics becomes more complex the longer you ponder them. However, nowadays a company would take action long before such a situation arose. No supplier would be so over-dependent on your order, the organisation would help the supplier to improve their business practice, and a decent period of notice is written into the contract. Thus both the organisation and the supplier are protected.

Heller also quoted a survey done by Raymond Baumhart, a Jesuit priest, in the 1960s. Of the 1,800 businessmen surveyed, no fewer than two-thirds rated their own companies 'more ethical than industry average', which makes for a rather interesting average. Five out of every nine, however, thought that businessmen would violate a written code of ethics whenever they thought they could avoid detection.

Heller thought that the biggest category of unethical conduct occurs when someone acts in pursuit of material gain, either for the company or themselves, which in ordinary circumstances would be classified as theft. He argued that being ethical can in some circumstances be part of giving the customer a quality product. Indeed, we rely on our choice of supermarket, Marks & Spencer, to ensure that the hens from their suppliers have a relatively happy life and we are content to pay a premium for them to do that.

The ethics industry

In 1988, when Conference Board, a business research group, held its first ethics conference, it found only one delegate with the word 'ethics' in their job title. In 2005, 1,200 ethics officers in over 500 companies were members of a professional ethics organisation.[3] In fact, the number of ethical scandals, such as Enron and WorldCom, seems to have risen to correlate with the number of ethics officers. There is also an Institute of Business Ethics. Lord Woolf has been chosen to chair a committee that will investigate BAE Systems' ethical standards following allegations of bribery and corruption. Under the terms of reference Lord Woolf (a former chief judge of England and Wales) will investigate only current and future ethical policies and procedures.[4] His brief thus excludes the bribery allegations surrounding the Al Yamamah contract with Saudi Arabia.[5] The fact that the contract was with Saudi Arabia raises issues about national culture, discussed in Chapter 7. In some countries, helping third parties to gain lucrative contracts by acting as a go-between must be rewarded, as the contact is able to use his/her talents to bring parties together. What is and is not acceptable in different cultures is also an issue in the case of the disciplinary hearings of Marta Andreasen, the European Commission's former chief accountant.[6] In 2005 she revealed the chaotic state of the

Commission's budgets, which she tried to reform, only to be sacked for her endeavours, having stood up against too many vested interests. On the larger stage, business ethics are related to corporate governance. In ethics much must rely on the individual values of the members of the ethics committees and their understanding of the world they operate in.

The roots of ethics go back to the Greek philosophers, and particularly to Aristotle, who wrote:

> Virtue is a state of character concerned with choice, lying in a mean, i.e. the mean relatively to us, this being determined by a rational principle, i.e. by that principle by which the man of practical wisdom would determine it.[7]

In other words, ethics are relative. Aristotle also said that the aim of an enquiry into ethics is not knowledge but action,[8] which is probably not new to a cultured man like Lord Woolf.

Some of the best-known examples of business ethics were demonstrated by the Quakers, whose beliefs certainly affected the way they did business and treated their employees. Trade beckoned Quakers because many other routes to self-advancement were blocked – inheriting as they did no great estates, barred from Parliament and universities, ineligible for the armed forces because of the Peace Pledge, and avoiding anything simulated and insincere such as the theatre. As they were fair in their dealings and did not charge rapacious interest they particularly prospered in banking. (By 1826 there were 74 Quaker banks, including Lloyds and Barclays.) They also made their mark in chocolate from the early 1800s – hence Fry, Rowntree, Cadbury, and Barker & Dobson, to name but a few. Many factory villages, such as Port Sunlight, Cadbury and Saltaire, were influenced by Quaker thought. However, lest we think that the Quakers were saints, Joseph Rowntree is said to have filched his rivals' recipes, there was no employee sick pay for venereal disease, and no honeymoon if the bride was already with child. Nowadays we would call it paternalistic, but in its day it was profoundly forward-thinking and benevolent, even if in many ways what the Quakers did was merely to apply sound business principles.[9]

Personal freedom versus society's rules

Personal freedom is at the root of ethics and the problem that lies at the heart of ethical decisions. In the Introduction to Iris Murdoch's *Sovereignty of Good*,[10] D. Z. Phillips says that Murdoch challenges existentialist and Kantian assumptions concerning personal freedom, and:

> suggests a more modest, and as she believes, more realistic picture of moral endeavour, as the attempt to overcome illusions and selfish fantasy in order to see and respond to the real world.

This is very reminiscent of van der Molen's argument (given in detail in Chapter 2) concerning individual assertiveness and the craving for social affiliation, a conflict with which all human beings struggle.[11] It also brings to mind our finding that most people's best examples of teams were those from outside work. One of the issues, presumably, is that there is less conflict about values and ethical choice. There is always a problem concerning personal freedom at work. The role of the organisation is to align its members along the lines it wants to go. As soon as these two diverge it has lost the complete focus of individual energies. Decisions and problem-solving are always made in respect of some other identity (i.e. the organisation), as well as one's own, to a greater or lesser degree.

The Parable of the Sadhu

Unfortunately, ethics has a stable-door quality about it. The time to discuss what you are going to do in an emergency is before that emergency arrives, as they usually do, without warning. When trouble strikes everyone is too busy trying to save themselves to act in the interests of a business or group. The time for joint action is past. That is why McCoy's 'Parable of the Sadhu' is so illustrative in this context.[12]

The multinational members of the group in this story were not a team in any exact sense of the word. They were individuals who found themselves with the same goal, facing an unexpected life-and-death situation. However, they do demonstrate what happens when there is no understanding of each other's ethical position. The Executive Summary starts:

> When does the group have responsibility for the well-being of an individual? And what are the differences between the ethics of the group and the ethics of the individual?

The action took place in the Himalayas. Meeting a *sadhu* (a Hindu holy man) on their way to attaining the highest point of their climb in 1983, McCoy's fellow climbers immediately wrapped him in warm clothing, took him part-way to a village, left him, and resumed their climb. No one knows what happened to the *sadhu*. Almost within touching point of the culmination of their dreams, the group was unprepared for this dilemma and, having done what they thought was a reasonable amount of caring, was not organised enough to take any further responsibility for him. The factors in this situation were complex. The group was tired; they were suffering from altitude sickness; helping the man any more than they had done would have prevented some, perhaps all of them, reaching the summit; the burden on the sherpas, whose living it is, would have been intolerable.

McCoy says that at the time he had a high adrenaline flow, a super-ordinate goal and a once-in-a-lifetime opportunity. These are also common factors in some corporate situations such as mergers, acquisitions and takeovers, and are highly stressful. The two situations are not as far apart as the geography might lead us to believe.

The questions McCoy continued to ask himself, long after the event, were 'Is there a collective or constitutional ethic that differs from the ethics of the individual?' and 'At what level of effort or commitment can one discharge one's ethical responsibilities?' He says:

> Not every ethical dilemma has a right solution. Reasonable people often disagree – otherwise there would be no dilemma. In a business context, however, it is essential that managers agree on a process of dealing with dilemmas. Because the group did not have a set of pre-conditions that could guide its actions, we reacted instinctively as individuals. The cross-cultural nature of the group added a further layer of complexity.

He believes that:

> Organisations that do not have a heritage of mutually accepted, shared values tend to become unhinged during stress, with each individual bailing out for himself or herself. Because managers have to deal with risk they need the guidelines of an agreed-upon process and set of values within the organisation.

One of the points of this *sadhu* story is that the group were just that – a group. If a group are to become a team this is just the sort of dilemma they need to solve when they are setting out, especially if they are a group which will be dealing with uncertainty. There is also a cultural aspect to this story which relates to the chapter on national culture (Chapter 7). McCoy has visited many institutions and business schools with this story. Hindu business people have told him that in trying to assist the *sadhu* he was being a typically arrogant Westerner imposing his cultural values on other parts of the world. (Other members of the group were from New Zealand and Japan.) They point out that the head sherpa's responsibility was to get his group up and down the mountain safely. His livelihood and status in the sherpa ethnic group depended on that. Any different action by the group would have put him in jeopardy, although his concerns seem hardly to have been addressed by the group. In conclusion, the group was forced to make a group decision, not an individual one. Everyone would have had to sacrifice their dreams for the *sadhu*.

Information and research on teamwork and ethics is thin on the ground. In Megone and Robinson's *Case Histories in Business Ethics*,[13] one of the case studies is about NASA and its partners. The problems with the seals which caused Challenger Flight 51-L to leak fuel and explode were between teams rather than within teams, and illustrate the role of hierarchies:

> the management structure in the key organisations was fragmented and divisive leading to crucial safety data not being collected or properly appreciated.

Such was the antagonism between groups that individuals put their own need for self-aggrandisement before the needs of the astronauts, who were totally dependent upon them for their safety. This is perhaps an area where we do not perhaps think of ethics – where the safety of others depends on our ethical dealings with one another in the team.

Problems with whistle-blowing

Sissela Bok has some useful things to say about individuals in teams.[14,15] Her three key terms are 'dissent', 'breach of loyalty' and 'accusation'. An individual has to disagree with the actions of the other members of the team and breach the code of loyalty by revealing the problem, and of necessity is forced to accuse someone or a group of wrong behaviour. Bok talks about the 'close bonds of collegiality', particularly among professionals, where the prevailing ethic requires, above all else, loyalty to colleagues and to clients. This seems to act as a hallucinogenic fog, which blinds people to the true state of affairs. The person who does the dissenting and accusing is now known as a whistle-blower and very few of them are ever truly thanked for their pains. In the Bristol Hospitals baby deaths case, where the mortality rate for baby heart surgery was significantly higher than elsewhere, the causes were repeatedly explained away by the surgeons, despite the concerns of a paediatrician and a specialist charity worker who was a trained nurse. Eventually there was an inquiry, but not before the paediatrician had been forced to emigrate and the nurse to leave the Health Service.

It is not that individuals do not have ethics; it is that they are, on occasion, misdirected. When professional pressure allies with our desire for affiliation it is very difficult to stand up and be counted. So teams have to be ready for this and lay down the rules early on in their existence. Why is it that more women whistle-blow than men? Are men more professionally focused? That people will in general be obedient to authority was amply demonstrated by Milgram's infamous obedience experiments,[16] which appear to show how easy it is for some people to deny their responsibility to others.

In 1999, Britain introduced the Public Interest Disclosure Act as a result of several rail disasters in the late 1980s and early 1990s, where there was a suspicion that companies had stifled employees who had raised legitimate concerns about illegal and unsafe practices. Now, however, the law is being used by disgruntled executives, who are likely to get much bigger settlements for unfair dismissal and wrongful dismissal claims if they bolster their claims with whistle-blower allegations. This has resulted in one lawyer stating that most of the whistle-blower claims he had seen had come from people 'motivated by trying to line their pockets rather than high-lighting any alleged wrong-doing'. Other lawyers referring to the London financial district say that numerous employees in the City face reprisals for blowing the whistle and that there is an unfortunate culture in the City of shooting the messenger rather than dealing with the problem.[17]

Teamwork and ethics

An article by Miller and Thomas concerns teamwork and ethics.[18] They suggest that one result of empowerment and teamwork has been reduced hierarchical control mechanisms. They write:

> In the light of recent ethical scandals there is considerable concern regarding the effectiveness of the control systems of these more recent designs. The purpose of the study was to examine the reporting of unethical behaviour when in a teamwork condition as compared to peer or subordinate conditions. Participants were presented with work scenarios and asked to make decisions about whether or not to report the unethical act. Main effects and interaction effects were found indicating that reporting behaviour was impacted by relative position and relationship closeness.

This seems to indicate that people felt worse about complaining when in a team than when in a hierarchy. This would appear to be bad news for the ethicalness of teams. Perhaps teams have taken over from professional bodies in some situations, showing yet again the need for affiliation.

Most vast fortunes have been built on what we would now think of as unethical business dealings. During the late nineteenth and early twentieth centuries the American financiers were regarded as nothing more than brigands by their counterparts in London.

Morgan's adventures on the railroads and Kennedy's in real estate and bootlegging would not fit many current ethical policies. They were entrepreneurs with an eye for a deal who ran the companies they gave their names to like the autocrats they were, but could they exist now? Are Enron and WorldCom examples of individuals who didn't know when to stop, then found themselves in such a hole that they had to keep up with their pretences until the whole edifice came down around them? Or was there a whole team of people turning a blind eye or condoning what they were doing? What about Mr. Stonecipher, who was ousted as Chief Executive of Boeing in 2005, following an extramarital affair with an employee? Mr Stonecipher seems to have been rather unfortunate. Having taken over as the CEO after a spate of business scandals at Boeing, he boosted the share price by over 50 per cent in a year, as well as introducing the new code under which he was fired. Newspapers at the time thought that the judgement was puritanical and that it marked a shift from professional to personal ethics.[19] Clearly the rest of the board at Boeing did not think the same. Here the team were as one in believing that their man had to be whiter than white.

At the time of writing Conrad Black, the ex-CEO of Hollinger International is appealing against being found guilty of three counts of mail fraud and one of the obstruction of justice.[20] He was accused of siphoning off money from the company for his own personal needs. His defence was that his fellow board members knew all about it and anyway, nobody said anything at the time. The inference is that he was worth it. In fact this aspect of ethics, that you are using company time and/or resources to fulfil your personal needs, cuts deeply into many organisational layers. One Alex cartoon in the *Daily Telegraph* has two women crooning over a particularly fashionable handbag whose hallmark is that the owner's name is embroidered on it in the giver's handwriting – only, of course, its Alex's secretary's handwriting that is on his wife's new handbag. There are as many secretaries who resent having to do personal things such as gift-buying as there are those who love the secret power it gives them. The reason given is that the executives concerned are so busy giving all their time to the organisation that they don't have time like the rest of us to carry out those acts of birthday, anniversary and Christmas remembrance. If you use other members of staff to run your errands perhaps you should pause to think how ethical your behaviour really is. Do other members of your team do it? Should you discuss it and decide on a policy? At a much lower scale, do members of your team habitually take the firm's stationery and think nothing of it? Sometimes, people see this as payment in kind for their extra unpaid efforts. A friend of ours told us a story about doing some presentation work for a large oil company. She takes her own flipboard and whiteboard pens with her. On this occasion she accidentally took one of the company's pens in place of one of her own. Almost immediately someone from the company challenged her with having taken one of their pens. Luckily she was able to point out that it was a mistake on her part. This company had a very strong policy about equipment, especially of the 'walkable' variety.

Perhaps many people don't comment on another's unethical behaviour because they themselves are the beneficiaries of not necessarily unethical but 'kindly' acts. Plus of course the fact that many people can be so charismatic or powerful that no one opposes them. Robert Maxwell comes to mind here. This is the man who created the Pergamon Press in Oxford followed by a publishing empire culminating in the purchase of the *Daily Mirror* newspaper and was subsequently found to be using that paper's pension fund for his own purposes. Living in Oxford as we do, we hear about his many acts of kindness. This is little consolation, however, if you were a *Mirror* pensioner and have no pension today.

Where do values end and ethics begin, and vice versa? Ethics are a code of behaviour which dictates how the organisation regulates the way it goes about its business and relates to business issues, particularly how the organisation should behave towards suppliers, customers, competitors and employees. It is about protecting the good name of the organisation and its employees. For example, many organisations now have rules about the giving and receiving of presents and put a limit on the amount that a supplier or customer may pay for a gift for someone in the organisation. Sexual harassment and bullying are areas where ethics policies seem to be very relevant, although there is some doubt how useful they are when one sees the number of court cases on these topics. Values are much more about individuals and how they should behave towards each other. Clearly there is overlap, but at the edges the two are obviously different.

Someone has to set the tone on these issues, and that is usually the top team in any institution and organisation, although anywhere in the organisation can set standards. The Spanish drug investigation just before the 2006 Tour de France meant that nine riders, including three favourites, were withdrawn, because of their reported drug use. The *International Herald Tribune* reported that the twenty teams enrolled in the Pro Tour schedule of competition met and

> decided that any team not enforcing the overall code of ethics will not be allowed to race. Since that code excludes from competition any rider under investigation, it could affect dozens, if their names are made public in the Spanish Case.[21]

So in this case, does it mean that the teams themselves (involving not only riders but their managers) have taken the decision? Clearly, on some occasions it has been the medical side of the team's management that has been administering the drugs, but no one knows how much of this has been previously done in secret, or with the full knowledge of the team management. Do members of the team simply condone the practice, turn a blind eye, or think that it is none of their business what another rider does? People must know what is going on, but they have certainly not acted as a team with one voice. The tension between winning for oneself and winning for the team is a strong one in competitive cycling, especially at the level of the Tour de France, and once again serves to reinforce our motif throughout this book of the struggle between wanting to be part of society and wanting to do things your own way, with extra complications! In the event, as we now know, many riders left the Tour de France during the 2007 event under suspicion of doping, including the Yellow Jersey, Michael Rasmussen, whose alleged misdemeanours included the apparent missing of 'out of competition' doping tests, and the whole of the Cofidis team. However, the overall verdict seems to have been that while in the past riders objected to the doping tests and there was an element of team pressure to boost performance by any means available, now the reverse is true and the riders feel that tests are finding the culprits and there is pressure on the team to be clean. Here is an example where the feelings of the whole team had to be the same in order for progress to be made. What seems to have happened is that a whole echelon of young riders who do not want to be associated with drugs, and some like David Millar who have been involved and now are converts to the other side,[22] are coming to the fore and their views are prevailing. It shows the power of team ethics.

Summary

What we have done in this chapter is spend more time than in the other chapters in developing a case and persuading you that ethics can begin with any team no matter where they are in the hierarchy, although it is tempting to believe that ethics is a part of corporate governance and therefore only of interest to teams at the very top of an organisation. In other words, 'nothing to do with us'. If your team involves the personal safety of members of the team or of others then your ethics could be critical and a lack of them could have disastrous results. If you were to know that another member of your team cut corners or avoided their responsibilities by 'knocking off' early, would you feel responsible if there was an accident, for example on the railway? If some helpless person on your team is being bullied or harassed do you think that they should be able to take care of themselves? Perhaps you don't see them as a team member because they are too junior or unimportant? If someone on your team is the worse for alcohol or drug abuse for part of their working life, are you protecting them or covering up for them out of a misguided sense of loyalty? Are you afraid to whistle-blow because you are quite a lowly member of your team? All these situations represent an integral part of the content of this chapter. It is sometimes very difficult to do anything at all and sometimes ethics are misdirected. Alternatively, perhaps it would be better for your team to get a handle on this before anything happens.

In the next chapter we examine the power of technology, its history, its social aspects and, particularly, its effect on virtual teams.

What can you do about the power of ethics?

- Raise the issue of ethical behaviour with your team by putting it on the agenda of your next team meeting.

- Ask the team what ethics means to them and have a discussion about their individual views on it.

- Discuss with your team their current practices that seem to you to be borderline when it comes to ethics.

- Discuss with your team whether or not there are circumstances when the behaviour of the team could affect the safety or health of other teams in your organisation or the public outside it. If so, should you have some way of safeguarding this ethical responsibility?

- If you have a company ethical policy you can discuss its contents, ensuring that everyone understands it and what it means to you as a team.

- Ask the team whether they think that the company's ethical policy could or should be strengthened by a team ethical policy relating to your behaviour to one another.

Notes

[1] Clarke, E. (2007) 'Stop thief!', *People Management*, 8 Feb.

[2] Heller, R. (1987) 'Ethics in business', *Business Life*, British Airways in-flight magazine, Feb./Mar.

[3] *The Sunday Telegraph*, 5 Mar. 2005.

[4] *The Daily Telegraph*, 16 Jun. 2007.

[5] ibid.

[6] *The Daily Telegraph*, 15 Mar. 2005.

[7] Aristotle (trans. D. Ross) (1998 [*c.*350BCE]) *The Nichomachean Ethics* (Oxford: Oxford University Press).

[8] Megone, C. and Robinson, S. J. (eds) (2002) *Case Histories in Business Ethics* (London: Routledge).

[9] Walvin, J. (1997) *The Quakers, Money and Morals* (London: John Murray).

[10] Murdoch, I. (1970) *The Sovereignty of Good: Studies in Ethics and the Philosophy of Religion* (London: Routledge & Kegan Paul).

[11] van der Molen, 'Adaption-Innovation and changes in social structure'.

[12] McCoy, B. H. (2003) 'The parable of the Sadhu', *Harvard Business Review on Corporate Ethics* (Boston, MA: Harvard Business School Press)

[13] Megone, C. and Robinson, S. J. (eds) (2002) *Case Histories in Business Ethics* (London: Routledge

[14] Bok, S. (1984) *Secrets: On the Ethics of Concealment and Revelation* (Oxford: Oxford University Press).

[15] Bok, S. (1980) 'Whistleblowing and professional responsibilities', in D. Callahan and S. Bok (eds) *Ethics Teaching in Higher Education* (New York: Plenum Press).

[16] Milgram, S. (1974) *Obedience to Authority: An Experimental View* (London: Tavistock).

[17] *International Herald Tribune*, 19 Jun. 2007.

[18] Miller, D. and Thomas, S. (2005) 'The impact of relative position and relational closeness on the reporting of unethical acts', *Journal of Business Ethics*, vol. 61, no. 4, Nov.

[19] *The Sunday Telegraph*, 5 Mar. 2005.

[20] *CBC, Ca News Online*, Aug. 2007

[21] *International Herald Tribune*, 19 Jun. 2007.

[22] *Guardian Online*, 26 Jan. 2006.

10

The Power of Technology

Introduction

This chapter is about the power of technology. It addresses not only how the different attitudes and responses to technology of the individuals in a team can both help and hinder the effectiveness of the team's problem-solving, but also how different technologies can themselves affect how your team behaves, both inside and outside work.

It may surprise people to learn that technology has any effect on how a team operates, but it certainly does, and as technology gets more and more complex and globalised so the effect will increase. Communication is at the heart of teamwork and technology has increased the ways in which members of teams can communicate with one another, sometimes intruding into what might previously have been seen as one's personal life. Conversely, technology has made it easier to blur the boundary between working life and personal life so that people conduct their private interactions much more openly in the work setting. When everyone worked in the same workplace it wasn't difficult to communicate with a colleague face to face, as and when required. Not everyone is temperamentally suited to these interruptions and distractions, but in an office setting it is probably difficult to avoid them. Teams working at a distance have similar issues to work through, including the different types of technology that can be used to aid communication and their capacity for instant response. Below, we briefly explore some early examples of the effect of technology on work in organisations before turning our attention to its effects specifically on team working.

The beginning of understanding

Joan Woodward was one of the first people to make a study of the relationship between technology and organisation design.[1] From her work with companies in Essex in the late 1950s she deduced that those organisations whose structures were in line with the norm for their technology (unit production, small batch and continuous production) were likely to be the most effective. As management research is predominantly about observing what is happening and then making sense of what entrepreneurs know makes money, it probably did not come as much of a surprise to the successful factories, but it may have been a surprise for the unsuccessful. Technology affected work to the extent that there were more successful and less successful ways of being organised, depending on what was being produced. If you were a team working in the appropriate technology for your industry you had a much easier job to do than if you weren't.

Socio-tech

Shortly after the publication of Joan Woodward's seminal paper, the Tavistock Institute published research based on its work in the Durham and Northumberland coalfields and then later in India. This research built on that of Bion,[2] whose work with shell-shocked soldiers produced new insights into the dynamics of leaderless groups – fight/flight, pairing, etc. Members of the Tavistock Institute established a reputation for looking at the relationship between social behaviour and technology, coining the phrase 'socio-tech'.

'To cavil', according to the dictionary, means 'to make empty, frivolous objections', but in the Durham and Northumberland minefields of the 1950s it was the system of 'cavilling' which kept the mines operating. 'Cavilling' was a unique system, which in theory ensured the equitable sharing of workplaces in the mine, so that every group had an equal chance of working in good and bad conditions. In fact cavilling in practice did not ensure equal sharing of good and bad, but it did safeguard against favouritism and victimisation by the mine bosses and foremen. That this was thought necessary indicates the state of post-war relations between the miners, the unions (lodges) and the management. This traditional method of self-selection of work-teams overseen by the lodges strengthened internal rapport within teams. For example, if a man was not a good worker, his team mates knew this about him (he may have been someone's brother or uncle, have an illness or injury, or a large dependent family) and were prepared to tolerate this for the sake of good community relations and whatever compensation they could get from it. Better to have a man working than have to support his family. In single place working, where a multitude of skills were employed, this was wholly an advantage, but on the introduction of what is called the 'long-wall method' it had disadvantages. The conditions encountered on the long wall, where the work was sequential in terms of skills, proved too much for teams, which had no experience in organising themselves in the new way that long-walling demanded, and where the majority of the team members were unused to one another.

On the basis of this study[3] and others, the Tavistock researchers highlighted the importance of:

1. The need to optimise and bring together social and technical systems.

2. The importance of self-managing groups.

What the long-wall study highlighted is that people are prepared to discount co-workers' shortcomings, if they know and understand them. There may be a trade-off outside work, which involves material benefits or peace and harmony at home. This outcome led in turn to the concept of self-managed work groups,[4] which reached their apogee in the Scandinavian car industry. The numbing effects of the production line were ameliorated by small decision-making groups focused on the output of one thing. Perhaps the reasons mentioned in an earlier chapter commenting on the feminine culture of Scandinavia, and its focus on quality rather than quantity (Chapter 7), account for this phenomenon. Now, a combination of robotics for the most repetitive tasks, varied work and the production line seems to be the norm in most factories. This is significant for teams working together, as the technology is adapted to suit the work of the team and to enable them to manage their own production.

We have given these two examples to demonstrate that teams and technology have a history, but feel that the above is sufficient to make the case for the importance of technology in an industrial setting. In the office, by contrast, the effects of information technology (IT) within teams have not been so obvious, and that is what we now want to concentrate on.

Technology in the office

Enid Mumford has written extensively about the relationship between computers and people and has devised both a technique and a philosophy, known as Effective Technical and Human Implementation of Computer-based Systems (ETHICS).[5] Underpinning the concept is the idea that future users of a new technical system should be able to participate in the design process and help create systems that are humanistic and friendly as well as efficient and effective. The theory, which was particularly relevant to mainframe computers, was that if people were involved in the design of the new systems they would enjoy increased job satisfaction as well as efficiency. In the twenty-first century, with personal computers, hot-desking and personal digital assistants (PDAs), these ideas have come to seem of their time. However, Mumford's was one of the few pieces of work which focused on the relationship between technology and people, and accorded it an importance which it does not seem to have had before or since.

In a whole book devoted to teams and technology in the public sector, Mankin *et al.* say that while technology cannot be the panacea for poor inter-organisational collaboration, effective use of IT can facilitate a team-based approach to public service and policy decision-making.[6] The emphasis is as much on teams using IT effectively in a collaborative way as it is on team members doing so. What this piece of research does is highlight the importance of communication between individual team members and access to the same material if there is going to be the possibility of joined-up thinking. This becomes more and more important with the advent of the virtual team. It is certainly true in, for example, local councils, where different departments will hold separate pieces of information on their clients, which need to be accessed if a quality service is to be delivered.

Technology and the virtual team

Most of the recent literature concentrates on the virtual team, technology, and its impact on organisations. In their article, perhaps now a little dated, on virtual teams, Townsend and DeMarie make the important point that this new form of team:

> will enable organisations to become more flexible by providing the impressive productivity of team-based designs in environments where teamwork would once have been impossible.[7]

Describing virtual teams they say that the major difference between them and other teams is that they are linked primarily through advanced computer and telecommunications technologies, including desktop video conferencing, collaborative software and internet/intranet systems. To that list one now might add the technological abilities of mobile phones with text-messaging and videoing and technology such as the PDA. Owing to flatter hierarchies, teams are much more geographically and/or organisationally dispersed, and may, owing to outsourcing, be in another organisation altogether. Team-based work systems enable team members across these sites to recapture the potential of team-based work. Townsend and DeMarie feel that such systems are particularly useful for teams that need to provide creative responses to rapidly changing market conditions. In terms of our argument they write:

> In addition to developing the hardware and software infrastructure for virtual teams, it is equally critical to develop the teams themselves and to develop employees who can effectively participate in this new environment. What is different about the technical team is the amount of technical training that is required to empower team members to function in the virtual environment. Learning to use all the traditional team in an environment where most interactions take place through a telecommunications medium is a critical challenge. This is particularly true since technology continues to evolve and reinvent itself at an ever-increasing rate.

They add that one of the greatest challenges will be the successful incorporation of valuable, technophobic personnel into the virtual team environment. We certainly have had experience of this, and later in this chapter we describe in some detail the effects of such people on a sophisticated IT project team.

As we mentioned in Chapter 6, on values, IBM had to reinvent itself in order to stay in business and is still having to do so. Over the years IBM has been challenged by disruptive waves of technology, from the minicomputer to the internet. Now, it sees the globalisation of services as the next big shift in the global landscape, and it is moving to adapt.[8] It is reinventing itself this time by moving up to the higher-value portions of the industry and creating a globally integrated enterprise. The trick for companies like IBM is to know what work to do where. The idea is to build networks for producing and delivering technology services much like the global manufacturing networks that have evolved over the last couple of decades. A utility project that IBM is currently running in Texas offers a glimpse of the global formula. The far-flung work team includes research scientists in Yorktown Heights, New York and Austin, Texas; software developers in Pune and Bangalore, India; engineering equipment and quality control specialists in Miami and New York; and utility experts and software designers who come from Philadelphia, San Francisco, Los Angeles, Chicago, North Carolina and elsewhere. However, there are limits to what technology can do at a distance. For those engineers whose work involves translating between the different vernaculars and cultures of computing and electric power, as they oversee the design and building of software tailored for utilities, the job has to be done face to face. Sometimes, IBM has recognised that the essential skill concerns business knowledge a lot more than it does software technology. Although the team is a virtual one, there are some parts of the task which require someone to be there co-ordinating it all the time.

Our rule when working with teams is that only work that could not be done via technology should be brought to face-to-face meetings. Time should be used appropriately at these meetings to network, interact and understand nuances and subtleties. The feeling of 'togetherness' after a meeting decays over time. We are human and need social interaction. What might be called a 'sniff' factor. What we found is that many team leaders could not resist the temptation to over-structure and fill the space in order to justify having the meeting in the first place. They were usually full of presentations that could just as easily have been sent over the internet. What was needed was the space for predictable but unplanned issues to erupt, which could then be tackled. Face-to-face meetings should be about discussion rather than information sharing.

To some extent, help is at hand in this respect – quite literally! Professor Nigel Shadbolt, president of the British Computer Society, has said that 'allowing people to feel directly what they are seeing on a computer screen is a Holy Grail'. Professor Alan Marshall of the Department of Electrical Engineering at Queen's University Belfast, who has been developing the 'haptic' or touch technology, believes it will make the internet a far more 'complete' experience.[9] He expects haptic devices to be commonplace within about five years, perhaps even replacing the computer mouse. If so, this would revolutionise communication between virtual team members.

Work life and social life

It is difficult to imagine a member of a coalmining team taking time out to answer their mobile phone. Members of the team would only communicate with each other and probably did very little of that until it was time to eat their Cornish pasty or whatever they had taken down the mine to eat. They did not spend much of their time in idle chatter while working, as this took up valuable energy or acted as a distraction in a dangerous environment. However, as explained above, the working group was also the social group. In offices, this was also the case until relatively recently. Many of you may still remember the embarrassment caused by having to take a personal phone call at work. Unless it was a life-or-death matter this was frowned on as interfering with your work and what you were paid to do. How times have changed! Now, people staring at computer screens are just as likely to be conducting social interaction with someone they hardly know, but who is part of their personal life, as communicating with work colleagues. This means, in effect, that at any time they are switching in and out of team cohesion. You may be sitting facing someone whose mind is not on you and your team problems at all. The team is certainly no longer the social unit – witness the demise of work social clubs. Team members have unlimited opportunities to interact outside the team owing to the growth of social networking. If you have members of your team of a certain age, probably under thirty-five, they will almost certainly be members of a system such as Facebook. Begun by the students at Harvard University as a way of keeping in touch with one another, this system has spread around the world. Members can use it to communicate with new friends and as a place to put personal information about themselves. In 2007 it was estimated that users of the system spent an average of twenty minutes a day on it,[10] but that has certainly been increasing with its widening popularity. Now, it is the focus of many research projects as organisations try to get to grips with its effects. Some companies' attempts to ban it have been challenged and they have had to reverse their decision in the face of worker hostility. Many team members may see using systems such as Facebook at work as a *quid pro quo* for their availability to technology outside work. This may put pressure on organisations to be more flexible about what they see as acceptable use of technology at work. Team members may be very diverse in terms of how they view social interaction in the workplace, with some prepared to tolerate and/or enjoy much more than others.

Another example of where technology might be seen as a source of intrusion rather than utility is in meetings and on courses. Some people insist on checking their emails and text messages while they are in a meeting, claiming that they are perfectly capable of listening to their colleagues and responding to the computer at the same time, and of giving both sufficient and equal attention. However, it is often as though someone has left the room. It is certainly a statement that 'I am too busy to give my team members my full attention; other things have for me at least equal priority.' We tend to get agreement from our groups before we work with them as to what is and what is not acceptable. Sometimes we all agree that there are urgent issues in the offing and some calls are necessary. In that case the person concerned leaves the room and takes the call outside. We want our team members to be seen to be giving each other 100 per cent attention. On one occasion we all agreed that if anyone's phone rang it would be put in a bucket of water. But no one's did.

Not wanting to communicate

It may be that some people do not want to communicate and therefore no amount of technology will make them do it. There are various reasons for this. One possibility relates to personal intellectual property rights. In most organisations knowledge is power but in some it is about your prestige, how much you get paid and your survival. Do you really want to share your hard-earned information with others? In a government agency we were working with, it was decided to improve customer service by using Lotus Notes. It was the responsibility of whoever took an enquiry, be it by telephone, email or letter, to log that transaction and its outcome on Lotus Notes so that everyone else could have access. However, some people saw this information as their own intellectual property rather like a little black book, and would not share it, preferring to keep their contacts to themselves. You could see how this might also apply to, say, recruitment consultants and salesman, whose contacts are very important to them. Many organisations have appointed information officers whose difficult task is to get members of the organisation to share information for the good of the whole. They have often found it a thankless task.

As we have shown in Chapter 3, on problem-solving, people like to get information in certain ways depending on how they are as people. Some like a face-to-face meeting and will jump on a plane at a moment's notice. Others like a telephone call or teleconferencing. People with a more adaptive style are more likely to want to consider any information communicated in their own time and would prefer an email, fax or report. This gives them a chance to collect their ideas before making a response, which makes them feel much more comfortable and in control.

Technology has blurred the boundary between private life and work, not only by the social interaction of team members with people outside work, but also by enabling team members to receive information at home, on holiday or wherever they may be. Gadgets such as the PDA mean that people are accessible everywhere. This phenomenon has implications for the work–life balance debate. When is home life sacrosanct? We know of at least one family where a Blackberry has been thrown down the lavatory, and not by the owner!

It is therefore important to select the technology that supports different ways of communicating and use online technology on the basis of how team members want to give and receive information as a team. There is no universally accepted method of giving and receiving information. There will be avid and reluctant users of all systems. We were working with a team who themselves were in the IT world and who had agreed at a meeting to use an instant messaging system such as NetMeeting, which is less intrusive than a phone call but more immediate than email. (You are not forced to reply immediately but you know that someone is there waiting for a response.) We later learnt through the coaching sessions that two to three members of the team had never communicated using the method the team had agreed upon. This really upset some team members, who thought (a) that they had an agreement and (b) that this was in the best interests of the team. Technology is only as good as the weakest link. In this case the team leader did not push it and it was not taken up as an issue. In some instances it is because people are not trained to use the particular technology and this has to be a consideration, but as these were all techie types this was not the case here. However, it does serve to highlight the point made above by Townsend and DeMarie.

Having an aversion to technology

Another aspect of an aversion to technology may relate to some work we have already looked at – that of Simon Baron-Cohen.[11] Baron-Cohen says that if there is an extreme male brain which processes or 'systemises' to excess there must in theory be an extreme female brain. Their empathising ability would be average or above-average in relation to the general population, but their 'systemising' would be impaired. These people (not necessarily women) 'would have difficulty understanding maths or physics or machines or chemistry, *as systems*'. Just as those with the extreme male brain experience a disability when they are expected to be socially able, those with the extreme female brain might only experience problems where the person is expected to be systematic or technical. The ability to use systems must be on a continuum, with those with the female brain being less likely to be technically minded and expert users of systems and computerisation. In addition, there will always be the factor of intelligence which will affect any innate ability one way or another. This is something to bear in mind if you find yourself as a leader becoming exasperated with those who seem unable to function in a way that makes sense to you, especially if they are of a more empathising nature. Baron-Cohen says that for many people there seems to be a trade-off, so that a higher ability in one process tends to be accompanied by a lower ability in the other process.

An IT case study

If you are the leader or manager or member of an IT team, you may feel that your reason for existence as a team is to provide the best technical expertise to your customers. However, the customers may not always want what is 'best', as is illustrated by this story, which involved some of our colleagues. Having purchased the rights to use an online questionnaire, our colleagues were unhappy to discover that without being consulted or their approval being sought they were being subjected by the originators of the questionnaire to several 'improvements' to the material whereby individuals had access to the results. Some of the improvements comprised much more complex diagrams, which meant that the size of the downloaded file had doubled from under 1Mb, which was acceptable to most firewalls, to over 2Mb, which was not. As our colleagues personally sent the downloaded file to each individual with whom they were in correspondence, this resulted in lost files of a very personal nature, and files that were not received in time. Our colleagues were very aggrieved about this. They were not getting what they were paying for and it was creating headaches for them. They were not appearing to give *their* clients the service that they prided themselves upon. As a result they felt forced to stop purchasing what had been a perfect instrument and use something else. In this case the 'improvements' had not been improvements for them at all, but had in fact been detrimental. It would not have been so bad if they had been given a choice, but it was the improvements or nothing. The supplier was not interested in going backwards. No one else had complained. We suspect that this happens quite often as the IT world tries to produce a better, slicker product and its customers would have been happy to stick with the old.

Time shifts

Working with team members from around the world means that their colleagues are aware of the window of opportunity for, say, talking to people in London, Chicago and Dubai at the same time. They plan their day so as to be available. With email this time-shift doesn't matter as the message is there waiting as soon as someone gets into work. However, time-shifts can have a highly destructive effect on the people who have to jet round the world. One UK organisation we know took over a Japanese company. (Yes, it does happen!) The CEO flew to Japan at least once a month to hold board meetings, but as he said, he was not sure how well he functioned when he got there. Not only was he acting in a diametrically different time pattern, but in a culture which was very different from his own. If members of your team have to do this regularly you might ask yourself what sort of decisions they are making as a result. On the other hand, time-shifts can keep your team working 24 hours a day. In small hospitals across America radiologists email CAT scans to Australia or India. When they come into work the following morning the analysis of the scan is waiting for them. Last century's disadvantage – the vast geographical distance – is this century's big plus. As Mark Steyn says, 'when it's moonlight on the Hudson, it's CAT-scanning time on the Ganges'.[12] Here time difference is being used as a benefit. Such differences have been used by the financial world spot markets for some time, but the rest of us are now catching up. All kinds of materials are shipped round the world to be processed, and the work done in different time zones, which means '24/7' works for the good of teams and organisations.

Summary

In this chapter we have looked at how technology first affected the work of teams in organisations, particularly the relationship between technology and social interaction. When communication in the team at work had repercussions on the social grouping outside work, changing the technology could affect those relationships adversely, sometimes leading to a complete breakdown, which then had repercussions in the workplace. Now, team members are just as likely to be conducting non-work-related social interactions in the office as work-related interactions with their colleagues, and the line between the two has blurred considerably. Some people find it difficult to use different types of technology because of how they like to deal with information and some are simply technology-averse. Such issues should be addressed by the team with regard to what, when left to their own devices, people really are going to do. On occasion knowledge is power and team members may feel deprived of what gives them standing and prestige. Sometimes it might be a question of inadequate training. Alternatively, there may be ways in which your team could become more efficient by using technology across time zones. If your team is involved with the use of technology for customers you may consider whether what you are changing is for the good of the customer or the team. And finally, there may be some jobs that do need to be done face to face and cannot be done by a machine, no matter how diverse the technology!

What can you do about the power of technology?

- Put the team's use of technology on the agenda of your team meeting and review it in terms of what you use and why, in relation to the task the team is doing. Could use technology more appropriately?

- Think about your team in terms of the technology used – are there some people who like some pieces of technology and not others? Could this be related to how they like to communicate?

- Are there people on your team who are technology-averse? Is this because of their psychological make-up, or do they genuinely not know what to do?

- Has your team agreed a course of action but there are members of the team who do not follow whatever was agreed? Do you enforce agreements strictly enough?

- Does your team have rules as to how much social interaction is acceptable in the office, at meetings and on courses? Is it adhered to? Should you raise it as an issue?

- Is your team using technology in a way that is good for the customer as well as the team?

- If your team is a virtual one, is it meeting frequently enough to form relationships conducive to the trust and openness which may be needed for solving some problems?

- Are there some parts of the job which really should only be accomplished face to face?

Notes

[1] Woodward, J. (1958) *Management and Technology* (London: HMSO).

[2] Bion, W. R. (1961) *Experiences in Groups and Other Papers* (London: Tavistock).

[3] Trist, E. L., Higgin, G. W., Murray, H. and Pollock, A. B. (1963) *Organisational Choice* (London: Tavistock).

[4] Benders, J., Huijgen, F. and Pekruhl, U. (2002) 'What do we know about the incidence of group work (if anything)?', *Personnel Review*, vol. 31, no. 3, pp. 371–85.

[5] Mumford, E. (1993) 'The ETHICS approach', *Communications of the ACM*, vol. 36, issue 3, Jun., p. 82.

[6] Mankin, D., Cohen, S. and Tora, K. B. (1996) *Teams and Technology: Fulfilling the Promise of the New Organisation* (Boston, MA: Harvard Business School Press).

[7] Townsend, A. and DeMarie, S. (1998) 'Virtual teams: technology and the workplace of the future', *Academy of Management Executive*, vol.12, issue 3, p. 17.

[8] Steve Lohr in the *New York Herald Tribune*, 5 Jul. 2007.

[9] Richard Gray in *The Sunday Telegraph*, 16 Sept. 2007.

[10] Facebook statistics.

[11] Baron-Cohen, S. (2004) *The Essential Difference* (Harmondsworth: Penguin).

[12] *The Spectator*, 16 Apr. 2005.

Epilogue

In this book we have put forward the following points:

1. Teams come in all shapes and sizes, and are there to solve problems in order to support the organisation.

2. Teams are expected to solve simple puzzles, complex puzzles and problems.

3. In this context, a problem has been defined as a situation where there is disagreement about whether or not a problem exists, the nature of the problem, and what the solution to the problem might be.

4. The more a team needs to share and pool information, which usually happens in times of change, the more uncertainty there will be.

5. This uncertainty around the nature of the problem is partly the result of the different perspectives and experiences of the team members. This diversity in approach to problems prevents the team from being as effective as it could be.

6. This diversity in approach is not the only factor that stops teams being as effective as they could be (there are others), but it is the one that we have been concentrating on in this book.

7. People often behave badly in teams because they are struggling both to find a voice of their own and to receive the approbation of their colleagues. If everyone can be valued, conflict can be reduced.

8. Diversity is a good thing if the problem-solvers can find ways of articulating their different approaches and experiences. It

enables a wider range of problems to be solved in a variety of ways.

9.   The problem lies in recognising these diversity factors and in finding languages with which to articulate them. An understanding of this essential tension enhances the effectiveness of the team, because it enables team members to be valued for what they have to offer.

10.   We have identified eight critical diversity factors:
   - problem-solving style
   - creative style
   - team role
   - values
   - national culture
   - masculine and feminine approaches
   - ethics
   - technology.

11.   We have suggested questionnaires and other methods, including exercises, to enable you to understand which of the factors may be holding your team back. You may now want to return to Exercise 1 (page 227) and use it as a benchmark to see if your team has changed in any way since you first started reading this book and applying its ideas.

We wish you every success with your efforts. If you succeed in accessing the diversity in your team, you will not only have made your team more effective; you will have supported your organisation in its endeavours and provided a healthy psychological environment for your individual team members, because their contribution is more valued.

Bibliography

Abraham, D. E. (1999) 'Facets of personal values: a structural analysis of life and work values', *Applied Psychology: An International Review,* vol. 48, issue 1, Jan., p.73.

Allport, G. W. and Vernon, P. E. (1931) *A Study of Values* (Boston, MA: Houghton Mifflin).

Anderson, N. and Sleap, S. (2004) 'An evaluation of gender differences on the Belbin Team Role Self-Perception Inventory', *Journal of Occupational and Organisational Psychology*, vol. 77, issue 3, pp. 429–37.

Aristotle (trans. D. Ross) (1998 [*c.*350BCE]) *The Nichomachean Ethics* (Oxford: Oxford University Press).

Ashby, W. R. (1956) *Introduction to Cybernetics* (New York: Wiley).

Barlow, N. M. (2006) *Re-think: How To Think Differently* (Chichester: Capstone).

Baron-Cohen, S. (2004) *The Essential Difference* (Harmondsworth: Penguin).

Belbin, R. M. (1981) *Management Teams: Why They Succeed or Fail* (London: Heinemann).

Bell, M. P., Gilley, K. M. and Coombs, J. (2003) 'Diversity at the top: effects of CEO and board member diversity on organisational diversity', paper presented at the Academy of Management meeting, Seattle.

Benders, J., Huijgen, F. and Pekruhl, U. (2002) 'What do we know about the incidence of group work (if anything)?', *Personnel Review*, vol. 31, no. 3, pp. 371–85.

Bilsky, W. and Schwartz, S. H. (1994) 'Values and personality', *European Journal of Personality*, vol. 8, pp.163–81.

Bion, W. R. (1961) *Experiences in Groups and Other Papers* (London: Tavistock).

Bohm, D. (1965) *The Special Theory of Relativity* (New York: Benjamin).

Bok, S. (1980) 'Whistleblowing and professional responsibilities', in D. Callahan and S. Bok (eds), *Ethics Teaching in Higher Education* (New York: Plenum Press).

Bok, S. (1984) *Secrets: On the Ethics of Concealment and Revelation* (Oxford: Oxford University Press).

Bouchard, T. J. (Jr), Lykken, D. T., McGue, M., Segal, N. L. and Tellegen, A. (1990) 'Sources of human psychological differences: the Minnesota study of twins reared apart', *Science*, vol. 250, no. 4,978, 12 Oct., p. 223.

Boyatzis, R. E., Murphy, A. J. and Wheeler, J. V. (2000) *Philosophy as a Missing Link between Values and Behaviour*, University of Waterhead, Cleveland, OH. Retrieved from Google Scholar, July 2005: http://ei.haygroup.com/   resources/ Library_articles/Philosophy%20as%20a%20Missing%20Link.pdf

Brown, M. (1988) *The Dinosaur Strain: The Survivor's Guide to Personal and Business Success* (Shaftsbury, Dorset: Element Books).

Bulmer, Michael, (2003), *Francis Galton: Pioneer of Heredity and Biometry*, John Hopkins University Press

Casey, D. (1985) 'When is a team not a team?', *Personnel Management*, Jan., pp. 26–9.

Cattell, R. B. (1957) *Personality and Motivation: Structure and Measurement* (Yonkers-on-Hudson, NY: World Book Co.).

Chartered Management Institute (2006) *Guidance for Managers: The Growing Importance of Diversity in the Workplace*.

Clarke, E. (2007) 'Stop thief!', *People Management*, 8 February.

Cox, T. H. and Blake, S. (1991) 'Managing cultural diversity: implications for organisational competitiveness', *Academy of Management Executive*, vol. 5, no. 3, p. 45.

De Bono, E. (1985) *Six Thinking Hats* (Boston, MA: Little, Brown).

Douglas, M. (1966) *Purity and Danger: An Analysis of the Concepts of Pollution and Taboo* (London: Routledge).

Egri, C. P., Ralston, D. A. *et al.* (2004) 'Managerial perspectives on corporate environmental and social responsibilities in 22 countries', *Academy of Management Best Paper Proceedings*.

Evans, R. and Russell, P. (1989) *The Creative Manager* (London: Unwin Hyman).

Evans-Pritchard, E. E. (1937) *Witchcraft, Oracles and Magic Among the Azande* (London, Faber & Faber).

Fisher, S. G., Hunter, T. A. and Macrossan, W. D. K. (1997) 'Team or group? Managers' perception of the difference', *Journal of Managerial Psychology*, vol. 12, issue 4.

French, R. (2007) *Cross-cultural Management in Work Organisations* (London: CIPD).

Gagné, R. M. (1974) 'Problem Solving and Thinking', *Annual Review of Psychology*, 10.

Gardner, H. (2007) *Five Minds for the Future* (Boston, MA: Harvard Business School Press).

Gibson, C. B. and Zellmer-Bruhn, M. E. (2001) 'Metaphors and meaning: an intercultural analysis of the concept of teamwork', *Administrative Science Quarterly*, June.

Goleman, D. (1995) *Emotional Intelligence: Why It Can Matter More than IQ* (New York: Bantam).

Hampden-Turner, C. and Trompenaars, F. (2000) *Building Cross-cultural Competence* (Chichester: Wiley).

Heller, R. (1987) 'Ethics in business', *Business Life*, British Airways' in-flight magazine, Feb./Mar.

Hertzberg, F. I. (1968) 'One more time, how do you motivate employees?', *Harvard Business Review*, vol. 46, issue 1.

Hofstede, G. (1981) *Culture's Consequences: International Differences in Work-related Values* (London: Sage).

Holden, C. (2007) 'See those fingers? Do the math', *Science Now*, May.

Honey, P. and Mumford, A. (1982) *The Manual of Learning Styles* (Maidenhead: Peter Honey Publications).

Horney, K. (1946) *Our Inner conflicts: A Constructive Theory of Neurosis* (London: Routledge).

Hunt, J. (1986) *Managing People at Work* (New York: McGraw-Hill).

Jackson, T. (2002) 'Reframing human resource management in Africa: a cross-cultural perspective', *International Journal of Human Resource Management*, vol. 13, issue 7.

Jackson, T. (2004) *International HRM: A Cross-cultural Approach* (London: Sage).

Jay, A. (1980) 'Nobody's perfect – but a team can be', *Observer Magazine*, 20 April.

Jonassen, D. H. (2000) 'Toward a Design Theory of Problem Solving', *Educational Technology Research and Development*, vol. 48, no. 4, Dec. (Boston, MA: Springer).

Jones, S. (2000) *The Language of the Genes* (London: Flamingo), 2nd rev. edn.

Kanter, R. M. (1983) *The Change Masters* (New York: Simon & Schuster).

Karakowsky, L., McBey, K. and Chuang, Y.-T. (2004) 'Perceptions of team performance: the impact of group composition and task-based cues', *Journal of Managerial Psychology*, vol. 19, issue 5, p. 506.

Katzenbach, J. R. (1997) 'The myth of the top management team', *Harvard Business Review*, Nov.–Dec., pp. 83–91.

Keay, J. (2000) *India, A History* (London: HarperCollins).

Kirton, M. J. (ed.) (1994 [1989]) *Adaptors and Innovators: Styles of Creativity and Problem-solving* (London: Routledge), rev. pbk edn.

Kirton, M. J. (2003) *Adaption-Innovation: In the Context of Diversity and Change* (London: Routledge).

Kolb, D. A. (1984) *Experiential Learning: Experience as the Source of*

Learning and Development (Englewood Cliffs, NJ: Prentice-Hall).

Koestler, A. (1967) *The Act of Creation* (New York: Dell).

Kreps, J. I. (2006) 'Anxiety', *Islamica*, 18.

Lessem, R. and Newbauer, F. (1994) *European Management Systems: Towards Unity out of Cultural Diversity* (London: McGraw-Hill).

Li, N. and Kirkup, G. (2007) 'Gender and cultural differences in Internet use: a study of China and the UK', *Computers and Education*, vol. 48, issue 2, Feb.

Litz, R. and Folker, C. (2002) 'When he and she sell seashells: exploring the relationship between management team gender-balance and small firm performance', *Journal of Developmental Entrepreneurship*, vol. 7, no. 4, p. 341.

Lucas, E. (2007) 'Making inclusivity a reality', *Professional Manager*, vol. 16, issue 4, July.

Luft, J. (1969) *Of Human Interaction* (Palo Alto, CA: National Press).

Malloy, F. (2006) 'A right earful', *Health and Fitness* (Australia), Jun.

Mankin, D., Cohen, S. and Tora, K. B. (1996) *Teams and Technology: Fulfilling the Promise of the New Organisation* (Boston, MA: Harvard Business School Press).

Mant, A. (1977) *The Rise and Fall of the British Manager* (Basingstoke: Macmillan).

Maslow, A. (1954) *Motivation and Personality* (New York: Harper).

McClelland, D. C. (1961) *The Achieving Society* (Princeton, NJ: Van Nostrand).

McCoy, B. H. (2003) 'The parable of the Sadhu', *Harvard Business Review on Corporate Ethics* (Boston, MA: Harvard Business School Press).

McGregor, D. (1960) *The Human Side of Enterprise* (New York: McGraw-Hill).

McManus, C. (2002) *Left Brain, Right Brain* (London: Weidenfield & Nicolson).

Mead, M. (1928) *Coming of Age in Samoa* (New York: William Morrow).

Megone, C. and Robinson, S. J. (eds) (2002) *Case Histories in Business Ethics* (London: Routledge).

Milgram, S. (1974) *Obedience to Authority: An Experimental View* (London: Tavistock).

Miller, D. (1990) *The Icarus Paradox: How Exceptional Companies Bring About Their Own Downfall* (London: HarperCollins).

Miller, D. and Thomas, S. (2005) 'The impact of relative position and relational closeness on the reporting of unethical acts', *Journal of Business Ethics*, vol. 61, no. 4, Nov.

Miller, D. and Karakowsky, L. (2005) 'Gender influences as an impediment to knowledge sharing: when men and women fail to seek peer feedback', *Journal of Psychology*, vol. 139, issue 2, pp.101–18.

Mumford, E. (1993) 'The ETHICS approach', *Communications of the ACM*, vol. 36, issue 3, Jun., p. 82.

Murdoch, I. (1970) *The Sovereignty of Good: Studies in Ethics and the Philosophy of Religion* (London: Routledge & Kegan Paul).

Nadler, D., Hackman, J. and Lawlor, E. (1979) *Managing Organisational Behaviour* (Boston, MA: Little, Brown).

Nemeth, C. J. (1986) 'Differential contributions of majority and minority influence', *Psychological Review*, vol. 93, pp. 23–32.

Nettle, D. (2007) *Personality: What Makes You the Way You Are* (Oxford: Oxford University Press).

Olofsson, G. (2004) *When in Rome or Rio or Riyadh: Cultural Q&As for Successful Business Behavior Around the World* (Boston, MA: Intercultural Press).

Page, Scott, E., (2007), *The Difference: How the power of diversity creates better groups, firms, schools, and societies,* (New Jersey: Princeton University Press).

Pavlov, I. P. (trans. G. V. Anrep) (1927) *Conditioned Reflexes: An Investigation of the Physiological Activity of the Cerebral Cortex* (London: Oxford University Press.)

Paxman, J. (1999) *The English: A Portrait of a People* (Harmondsworth: Penguin).

Petite, C. (1958) 'Le determinisme genetique et psycho-phisiologique de la competition sexuelle chez drosophila elangaster', *Bulletin Biologique*, vol. 92, pp. 248–329.

Renner, W. (2003) 'Human values: a lexical perspective', *Personality and Individual Differences*, 34.

Revans, R. (1980) *Action Learning: New Techniques for Management* (London: Blond & Briggs).

Robinson, S. (2002) 'Challenger Flight 51-L: a case history in whistleblowing', in Megone and Robinson (eds), *op. cit.*

Russell, P. (1979) *The Brain Book* (New York: Plume).

Schwartz, S. H. (1992) 'Universals in the content and structure of values: theoretical advances and empirical tests in 20 countries', in M. P. Zanna (ed.) *Advances in Experimental Psychology*, vol. 25 (New York: Academic Press).

Senge, P. (1993 [1990]) *The Fifth Discipline: The Art and Practice of the Learning Organisation* (London: Century).

Skinner, B. F. (1973) *Beyond Freedom and Dignity* (New York: Knopf).

Thomas, D. and Inkson, K. (2004) *Cultural Intelligence* (New York: McGraw-Hill).

Todorov, T. (trans. C. Porter) (1993) *On Human Diversity: Nationalism, Racism, and Exoticism in French Thought* (London: Harvard University Press).

Townsend, A. and DeMarie, S. (1998) 'Virtual teams: technology and the workplace of the future', *Academy of Management Executive*, vol. 12, issue 3, p. 17.

Trist, E. L., Higgin, G. W., Murray, H. and Pollock, A. B. (1963) *Organisational Choice* (London: Tavistock).

Trompenaars, F. (1993) *Riding the Waves of Culture: Understanding Cultural Diversity in Business* (London: Nicholas Brealey).

Tuckman, B. W. and Jensen, M. A. (1977) 'Stages of small group development revisited', *Group and Organisational Studies*, 2.

Van der Molen, P. P. (1994 [1989]) 'Adaption-Innovation and changes in social structure: on the anatomy of catastrophe', in M. J. Kirton (ed.) *Adaptors and Innovators: Styles of Creativity and Problem-solving* (London: Routledge), rev. pbk edn.

Vicere, A. A. (1991) 'The strategic leadership imperative for executive development', *Human Resource Planning*, vol. 15, issue 1, pp .15–31.

Walvin, J. (1997) *The Quakers, Money and Morals* (London: John Murray).

Watkins, J. M. and Mohr, B. J. (2001) *Appreciative Inquiry* (San Francisco, CA: Jossey-Bass/Pfeiffer).

Weber, E. (2006) 'Now hear this: differences in how men and women listen', *Vegetarian Times*, Nov.

Woodward, J. (1958) *Management and Technology* (London: HMSO).

Worman, D. (2006) 'Managing diversity is the business', *Impact: Quarterly Update on CIPD Policy and Research*, issue 17(1), Oct.

Worman, D. (2007) 'How fair are boardroom affairs?', *Impact: Quarterly Update on CIPD Policy and Research*, issue 19, May.

Exercises

Exercise 1. Does your team need help?

Answer 'Yes' or 'No' to the following questions. This exercise can be done at the beginning, before you read the book, and again when you have tried to put some of the ideas into practice. This should give you a benchmark to work from and show you whether or not you have changed things. You might also like to ask members of your team to complete it.

In the team:

1. Is there much unresolved conflict that affects the quality of problem-solving?

2. Do you feel that you are all working towards different objectives?

3. Are minority views ignored?

4. Is there plenty of camaraderie but not much trust and openness?

5. Are feelings ignored as not being part of the job?

6. Are decisions made by compromise?

7. Is there a feeling that some people are more 'creative' than others?

8. Are the people who have ideas rewarded but not those who carry them through?

Does the team:

9. Have a language with which to understand different points of view?

10. Develop a dialogue where ideas are exchanged rather than the loudest or strongest prevailing?

If you have answered a majority of numbers 1 to 8 with a 'Yes' and numbers 9 and 10 with 'No's', the likelihood is that your team needs help.

However, the amount of help it needs will depend on how much uncertainty there is in relation to the problems that the team solves and how much change it is going through. Only you can decide. You have the power.

Exercise 2. The diversity variables

Look at the following variables and decide which have had the most effect on the teams you have either led or been a member of. List them in order of priority.

Repeat this with your current team. What are the particular issues? Are there any diversity variables that you need to work on?

The eight diversity variables are:

1. Problem-solving style – how we approach, define and solve problems.

2. Creative style – we are all creative but with different styles, and we loosely divide into those who want to do things better and those who want to do things differently.

3. Team role – we each have a team role and they fit together (or not) to cover the team's work.

4. Values – our very basic reasons for doing things, which may not be good (cf. the Mafia and the Quakers).

5. National culture – approaching the way we work in terms of national cultural diversity.

6. Ethics – moral standards in business.

7. Masculinity and Femininity – differences between the masculine and the feminine in terms of the way we work.

8. Technology – communicating across distance and time zone.

Exercise 3. Categories A, B and C

Give some thought to identifying and noting down issues, problems, opportunities and/or challenges which apply to the following categories:

Category A.   This is the type of issue which, once it has been identified and it has been agreed that it requires attention, is within your individual core competency. Action requires little or no interaction with colleagues to carry out and therefore has little impact on the whole team's performance.

Category B.   This is the type of issue where you require some support and need to share some information with the team. It may be that one or more of the team members will have information you need as a result of current or previous experience. Therefore what you are doing will impact on all the team to some degree. Can you identify individually who those people might be?

Category C.   This is where you are uncertain or may have no idea what the answer might be, as you have not come across the issue as perceived before. You suspect that other members of the team may not know the answer either, but you do need to share a lot of information with them and work together if you are going to find a solution. Failure to do this will have a major impact on the team's effectiveness.

Once you have identified the issues that fall into each category, decide how you are going to deal with them.

Ask everyone in the team to do this exercise and compare notes.

Exercise 4. Co-operative groups and teams

Each person decides on a scale from 0 to 10 how your team behaves, with 0 being an Uncooperative Group, 5 a Co-operative Group and 10 a Team, using the lists of behaviours provided by Casey. We reproduce the lists below.

In a Co-operative Group:
- People work together.
- Commitment is high.
- Process issues are worked on covertly.
- People negotiate with each other.
- Information is passed on a 'need to know' basis.
- Conflict is accommodated.
- Politics are important.
- Feelings are not part of the work.
- Trust and openness are measured.
- Difficult decisions may be by compromise.

In a Team:
- People trust each other's judgement and behaviour.
- Feelings are expressed freely.
- Process issues are part of the work.
- Commitment is high.
- Objectives are common to all, and all people know them.
- Listening is high.
- Conflict is worked through: task is stopped where necessary.
- Decisions are by consensus.

Which of the two lists does your team feel applies to them in terms of their behaviour? Discuss these in depth. Where are you and where do you need to be? For example, are you currently clustered around 4 but need to move to 7? How will you close the gap?

Exercise 5. Choosing team values

Below are some examples of the values that we found when working with various groups and teams. Choose no more than eight of them as your core values or add your own. How do you think they affect your behaviour? How do they impact on your team?

Teamwork
Co-operation
Openness
Enjoyment
Partnership
Achievement
Developing people
Innovation
Courage
Trust
Safety
Fair day's work for a fair day's pay
Commitment
Integrity
Honesty
Accountability
Respect for the individual
Consistency
Face-to-face management
Forthrightness
Cross-functional working
Recognition and reward
Being valued
Creativity
Cost efficiency

Encouraging the new
People first
Quality
Customer focus
Growth
Empowerment
Profit consciousness
Pride in company
Encouraging change
Enthusiasm
Looking forward
Listening
Flexibility
Desire to change
Compassion
Hard work
Involvement
Loyalty
Making a difference
Highest ethical standards
Efficiency
Challenge
Environmental awareness
Action orientation
Fun

Repeat the exercise with your team. How will you go about bringing life to these values?

Exercise 6. Improving values

Write down your eight values from the previous exercise above a line as indicated below.

Then place a cross (x) to indicate where on the value scale you feel your team is at present, and place a circle (o) where you think they should be given the problems they are solving. Nought (0) is where the value is not lived at all and ten (10) is where the value is fully lived.

Then reproduce this exercise with your team.

You will probably find that every member of your team thinks differently on each value. Do not be dismayed. This is an opportunity to understand your team's thinking and to reduce some misunderstandings and conflicts which are holding your team back.

Value
0--------------------------------5----------------------------------10

How will you bridge the gap between where you and the team are and where you and the team aspire to be?

Appendices

Appendix 1.   Deva values

People within The Deva Partnership Ltd believe in:

- *Making a difference* – through effective change, positive growth and ownership.

- *Being valued* – for who we are and for what we do.

- *Enlivening spirit* – by encouraging individuals to discover the best in themselves.

- *Releasing energy* – by opening channels, encouraging flow and sustaining momentum.

- *Everyone being creative* – so that they have the ability to act.

- *Partnership* – by actively developing the relationship of working *with* not *for*.

- *Conscious learning* – by enabling the highest level of individual and team development to take place within an organisational context.

Appendix 2. Examples of Vision, Mission and Values

A leading international manufacturer of building products

Vision   We deliver on our promises.

Mission   Simpler, faster, better ... together.

Values   Respect, integrity, diversity, service.

The company's website states: 'Our vision, mission and values play a role in everything we do. The decisions we make, the interactions we have with customers and suppliers, the way we work with other departments ... all are shaped by vision, mission and values.'

Their definition of diversity is: 'To welcome the opinions and ideas of all people'.

Karuna

Karuna is a Buddhist organisation committed to human development and to challenging the ignorance and prejudice that trap people in poverty. '*Karuna*' is a Sanskrit word meaning 'compassionate action based on wisdom'.

Vision   A world without prejudice, in which every human being has the opportunity to fulfil their potential, regardless of their background or beliefs.

Mission   To enable the most disadvantaged children, women and men in South Asia to meet their needs, access their rights and participate in society.

Values   To express:
- the insight that all human beings are born with an equal potential for growth and development.
- tolerance, honesty and clear communication.
- professional competence and a commitment to education and learning.

Appendix 3. Examples of values in teams

A Shipbuilding Organisation

- Quality at price/cost/time.
- Profit-conscious.
- Satisfy customers.
- Management/self-accountability.
- People are valued.
- Career development.

This was written at a time when this company was moving from a system of cost plus to a budget with the MOD and there was a lot of belt-tightening coming up.

From an Instructor's Course

- Pride in work.
- Consistency in instructions and standards.
- Valuing the capability of the trainee.
- Accessibility to new ideas.
- Honesty and objectivity in feedback.

For Appraisal Courses

- Attitude is more important than knowledge and skills.
- Learning is by pooling experience in syndicates before being 'told'.
- Giving lots of realistic practice.
- Getting people out of activity into reflective observation.
- Getting people thinking more widely than the subject matter.
- Should be enjoyable.
- Giving people good experiences to build on.

Index